S. PAUL.
IN *S. DOMITILLA*.
4TH CENTURY.

Early Christians of Rome. Frontispiece.

EARLY CHRISTIANS OF ROME

THEIR WORDS AND PICTURES

BY
G. M. BEVAN, S.Th.
LICENSED TEACHER OF THEOLOGY

WITH A FOREWORD BY THE REV.
WALTER LOCK, D.D.
LADY MARGARET PROFESSOR OF DIVINITY IN
THE UNIVERSITY OF OXFORD

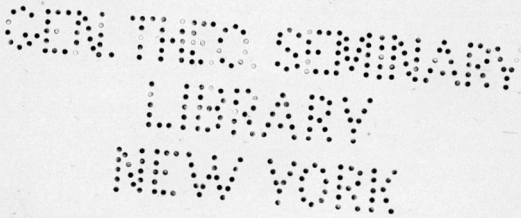

LONDON
SOCIETY FOR PROMOTING
CHRISTIAN KNOWLEDGE
NEW YORK AND TORONTO: THE MACMILLAN CO.

270.006
B467
83574

First published 1927

Printed in Great Britain

FOREWORD

I HAVE had the opportunity of reading this book in proof, and I am glad to wish it God speed. It is very readable and lucid and based upon a wide reading in the primary authorities on the subject with which it deals. It will be invaluable to the visitor to Rome who is making his first acquaintance with its Museums and Catacombs; but it is also of great value to any Christian wishing to understand the spirit in which the Christians of the first centuries faced the problem of converting a pagan world, and to realize the wide scope of their prayers and the richness of the doctrine by which they succeeded in their task.

WALTER LOCK.

CHRIST CHURCH,
  OXFORD,
    June 4, 1927.

PREFACE

THE purpose of this book is to offer some guidance to those who visit Rome with the desire of learning something of the Roman Church as it was in its earliest days. Many travellers coming to Rome for the first time have a sense of bewilderment amid the multiplicity of the unfamiliar sights around them. They may find themselves hurried through a Catacomb in a throng of sightseers, among the most precious monuments of Christian antiquity which they cannot stay to examine. And even in the clearer light and more leisurely progress through the great museums it may be almost as difficult to obtain any coherent comprehension of what is represented by the large number of objects displayed before them. Thus they may carry away no very clear idea of the significance of much that they have seen in Rome.

Those who desire to make a thorough examination of the subject have at their disposal many excellent books by archæologists who have devoted to this work many years of research. Such are the monumental works of De Rossi, Wilpert, and the *Dictionnaire d'archéologie chrétienne et de liturgie*, edited by Dom Cabrol. But there are many travellers who have neither time nor opportunity for any prolonged study, and to whom a visit to Rome is but a brief interlude in a busy life engaged in pursuits of a different kind. To such as these a small book

PREFACE

giving a brief outline of the significance of the monuments may be of some use; and possibly it may be not wholly without interest to some who have no opportunity of visiting Rome. For its aim is not to give the historical facts which can be found in any history of the Church in Rome, nor to take the place of the guide-books on the localities to be visited which most tourists possess. Its aim is to illustrate *from the remains of pagan Rome* the conditions of life in Rome in the days of the early Church, and thus to show how great were the difficulties which confronted her; and then to show *from monuments of early Christian Rome* what was the Faith of the multitude of the faithful which enabled them to face death with certain hope and invincible courage, and wherein lay its power to overcome the pagan world and to endure to the present day.

Most sincere thanks are due to Dr. Lock for his great kindness in reading this book in proof, and suggesting emendations, and for the approval of its aim which he has been so good as to express in the Foreword.

Note.—Of the inscriptions, some have been copied direct from the monuments in Rome; others will be found in the books mentioned in the Bibliography. A large number of Christian inscriptions has been arranged in the cloister of the Christian Museum of the Lateran, where they can be conveniently studied. An adjoining room contains Jewish inscriptions. This Museum also contains many Christian sarcophagi.

In the case of some of the inscriptions, paintings, and sarcophagi to which reference is made

PREFACE

in this book, an indication can be given as to where they may be found. But in some cases no such information is available; and even when the place is specified the possibility that certain objects may have been transferred elsewhere must be borne in mind.

The following Catacombs are open to the public:

S. Agnese, S. Sebastiano, S. Callixtus, S. Domitilla, S. Commodilla, S. Pancrazio.

To visit other Catacombs a special permit must be obtained from the Commissione di Archeologia Sacra. Piazza della Pigna, 14. S. Callixtus, S. Domitilla, S. Priscilla, and SS. Pietro e Marcellino, are of special interest.

CONTENTS

PREFACE v

CHAPTER I

IMPERIAL ROME IN THE DAYS OF THE EARLY CHURCH

S. Paul and S. Peter in Rome. The pride of Rome: the Imperial buildings . . . . pp. 1–7

CHAPTER II

THE PLEASURES OF ROME

The Colosseum. The Baths of Caracalla and of Diocletian
pp. 8–12

CHAPTER III

THE RELIGIONS OF ROME

The Temples of Vesta, Jupiter Capitolinus, Portunus, Mater Matuta. The Mysteries: the Temple of Cybele: the Temples of Mithra. The Mysteries and Christianity
pp. 13–21

CHAPTER IV

EARLY CHRISTIAN ROME

Jewish and Christian Catacombs . . pp. 22–26

CHAPTER V

CHRISTIAN SEPULCHRAL INSCRIPTIONS

pp. 27–33

CHAPTER VI

EARLY CHRISTIAN PICTURES ON SEPULCHRAL MONUMENTS

Their interpretation . . . . pp. 34–42

CONTENTS

CHAPTER VII
CHRISTIAN SYMBOLS
Symbols of Christ: the Good Shepherd, Orpheus, the Fish, the Dolphin. Meaning of the Orante.   pp. 43–51

CHAPTER VIII
SIGNIFICANCE OF SCENES FROM THE OLD TESTAMENT
The Garden of Paradise. The Four Rivers of Eden. The Creation of Man. The Fall. Noah and the Ark. The sacrifice of Isaac. Moses in the presence of God. Moses striking the Rock. Ascension of Elijah. Jonah. Job. Daniel. The Fiery Furnace. Susanna. Tobias

pp. 52–69

CHAPTER IX
SIGNIFICANCE OF SCENES FROM THE NEW TESTAMENT
The Mother of our Lord. The Magi. The Feast at Cana. The woman of Samaria. The paralytic. The feeding of the multitudes. The blind receiving sight. The raising of Lazarus. The denial of S. Peter. Pilate .   pp. 70–84

CHAPTER X
VARIOUS SYMBOLS
The Anchor. The Dove. The Hart. The Lamb. The Peacock. The Phœnix. The Ship . .   pp. 85–93

CHAPTER XI
THE SACRAMENTS
Baptism. Confirmation. The Eucharist .   pp. 94–104

CHAPTER XII
LATER CHRISTIAN ART
Christ enthroned. The Mosaics: S. Costanza, SS. Cosma e Damiano, S. John Lateran, S. Clemente. The Victory of the Faith . . . . . .   pp. 105–113

APPENDIX . . . . . .   pp. 114–115

BIBLIOGRAPHY . . . . .   pp. 116–118

LIST OF ILLUSTRATIONS

		PAGE
S. PAUL	*Frontispiece*	
S. PETER	*facing*	20
THE GOOD SHEPHERD . .	*facing*	44
THE EUCHARISTIC FISH .	. .	48
THE ORANTE . . .	*facing*	50
A CHRISTIAN SARCOPHAGUS .	*facing*	54
EUCHARISTIC SCENE . .	. .	97
EUCHARISTIC SCENE . .	*facing*	102
THE APSE AND TRIUMPHAL ARCH OF SS. COSMA E DAMIANO, ROME .	. .	109

For an explanation of the summary references in the footnotes, see the Bibliography.

References are given to Migne: *Patrologia Græca* and *Patrologia Latina*, as being the edition of the text most generally accessible.

EARLY CHRISTIANS OF ROME

THEIR WORDS AND PICTURES

CHAPTER I

IMPERIAL ROME IN THE DAYS OF THE EARLY CHURCH

S. Paul and S. Peter in Rome. The pride of Rome: the Imperial buildings

THE Roman poet [1] who sang the glory of Rome and prayed that the sun in his course might be able to gaze upon nothing greater than the city of Rome was but giving expression to the thought which rises in the mind of many a traveller as he wanders among the remains of the Imperial City. No words can convey the impression they produce, the overwhelming sense of the vastness, the splendour, the colossal strength of that great Empire, visible even in those broken fragments. The soaring arches and columns, the massive walls which have defied the ravages of eighteen centuries or more, represent a might which seemed as if it could never be shaken, a dominion which could endure through all time.

The Roman world as it was in the first centuries of our era rises before one's mind, and constantly the thought presents itself: It was

---

[1] Horace, *Carmen sæculare*.

into this world that there came the Christian message, first carried to the capital of the Empire by nameless Christians. Of their work no record survives, but from that obscure beginning there arose a Society endued with an imperishable life, and bearing the message which was powerful enough to change the Roman world. How was this possible in face of the forces arrayed against it ? That is the question which we ask again and again as we gaze upon what remains of Imperial Rome. And our thoughts travel back to a day in the spring of the year, perhaps A.D. 59, when a company of travellers from the East journeyed along that Appian Way which our feet still tread to-day, the road stretching across the vast and now desolate Campagna, and bordered with the ruins of ancient Roman tombs. It was the road which then led from the port of Puteoli to Rome. There were some Roman soldiers bringing their prisoner, who was accompanied by two of his friends, a Jewish teacher brought to Rome at his own desire in the hope of securing a more impartial trial than he had been able to obtain in his own country, to be tried in the Emperor's Court of Appeal.

The figure of S. Paul and that of S. Peter come continually before one's eyes in wanderings among the monuments of early Christian Rome. In the early tradition they always appear together. Though S. Peter is not mentioned in the letters written by S. Paul to and from Rome, there is a consensus of testimony in the writings of the early Fathers and others as to his work and his martyrdom in Rome.

IMPERIAL ROME

S. Clement, writing from Rome about A.D. 96, speaks thus:

Let us set before us the noble examples which belong to our generation. By reason of jealousy and envy the greatest and most righteous pillars of the Church were persecuted and contended even unto death. Let us set before our eyes the good Apostles. There was Peter, who ... endured not one nor two but many labours, and thus having borne his testimony went to his appointed place of glory. ... Paul by his example pointed out the prize of patient endurance. After that he had been seven times in bonds, had been driven into exile, had been stoned, had preached in the East and in the West, he won the noble renown which was the reward of his faith, having taught righteousness unto the whole world, and having reached the farthest bounds of the West; and when he had borne his testimony before the rulers, so he departed from the world and went unto the holy place, having been found a notable pattern of patient endurance. Unto these men of holy lives was gathered a vast multitude of the elect, who through many indignities and tortures ... set a brave example among ourselves.[1]

S. Ignatius in his Epistle to the Romans, § 4, about A.D. 110: " I do not enjoin you as Peter and Paul did." [2]

Dionysius, Bishop of Corinth, in his Epistle to the Romans (A.D. 170):

You have thus, by such an admonition, bound together the planting of Peter and of Paul at Rome and Corinth. For both of them planted and likewise taught us in our Corinth. And they taught

---
[1] Lightfoot, p. 7.   [2] *Ibid.*, p. 121.

EARLY CHRISTIANS OF ROME

together in like manner in Italy, and suffered martyrdom at the same time.[1]

S. Irenæus about A.D. 180 writes of "the greatest, most ancient, and well-known Church founded by the two most glorious Apostles Peter and Paul at Rome."[2]

Caius, a Roman presbyter writing early in the third century, says in a disputation concerning the places in which the bodies of S. Peter and S. Paul were laid:

I can show the trophies of the Apostles. For if you will go to the Vatican or to the Ostian Way, you will find the trophies of those who laid the foundations of this church.[3]

The time at which S. Peter first came to Rome cannot be determined with any certainty. But it is clear that there were Christians in Rome before S. Paul arrived there, since some of them came out to meet him (Acts xxviii. 15). And some three years earlier he had written to them: "Your faith is proclaimed throughout the whole world."

Thus S. Peter and S. Paul both laboured and suffered in Rome, and together they appear on the walls of the Catacombs, on the sarcophagi, and in the mosaics which adorn the ancient churches of Rome.

Apart from some examples of a conventional kind in which they appear beardless, as our Lord is also represented in the earliest days, there is a definite type by which the two Apostles

[1] Eusebius, *H.E.* ii. 25, 8.   [2] *P.G.* vii. col. 848.
[3] Eusebius, *H.E.* ii. 25, 7.

can be recognized. S. Paul is depicted with a
bald head, a lofty brow, a long nose, and a
rather long and straight beard; S. Peter with
a broader face, and curling hair and short beard.

For years S. Paul had longed to visit the
marvellous city. "I must see Rome." Had
Rome captured his imagination by her splendid
achievements in the cause of civilization, the
benefits of order and good government which she
had bestowed upon mankind, the vast extent of
her Empire, which embraced within its dominion
the most diverse races of the known world?
S. Paul was the first to grasp the full meaning
of that glorious vision of a yet wider dominion
which should gather into one men of every race,
and unite them, as even Rome had never united
her subjects, in a common, world-wide fellowship,
the Catholic Church.

And now at last S. Paul's longing to see Rome
was fulfilled. But how different was the fulfilment from that pictured by his eager expectation
(Rom. xv.), for he came as a prisoner in fetters.

What would he see as he entered its gates?
On the left hand rose the Palatine, crowned with
the palaces of the Cæsars. We may still see
masses of broken fragments of costly and many-coloured marbles which once covered their walls
and floors. Augustus could boast that he had
found Rome a city of brick, and had left it a
city of marble. On the banks of the Tiber he
built for himself a stately tomb in the form of a
lofty mound surrounded by marble terraces
and planted with cypress trees. His statue
crowned the edifice, and here his ashes were
laid, and those of the Cæsars who came after

him, and other members of the Imperial family. His palace on the Palatine is almost entirely buried under modern buildings, but the towering walls and arches still remain of the palace built some twenty-five years later by the mad Caligula. As time went on other palaces were added where the masters of the world held their court, and an army of officials carried on the administration of the vast Empire.

Below the Palatine lay that which had been for centuries the heart of Rome, the Forum. It was the meeting-place of the varied life of the city, the scene of business and of pleasure, of political meetings with a raised platform for the speakers, and another on which foreign ambassadors could stand and listen to the speeches. On one side rose the Senate House, and on the other the great Court of Justice built by Julius Cæsar, and hard by the lofty temple of Castor and Pollux founded in memory of the help which they were believed to have given the Romans in the battle of Lake Regillus, and near the temple was the pool at which the Twin Brethren washed their horses when they brought the news of the victory to Rome. Here also was the House of the Vestals, where the *Atrium Vestæ* still delights the traveller with its court and pools of water set about with roses and violets, whilst all around stand the stately forms of Vestals who once lived here in the enjoyment of the high honours accorded to them by the State.

The whole length of the Forum there ran the Sacred Way, along which passed the triumphal processions of victorious generals with captive kings and warriors in their train, up to

IMPERIAL ROME

the great temple of Jupiter Capitolinus, of which part of the massive wall has lately come to light. A few years later than S. Paul's time an arch of victory was built spanning the Sacred Way in honour of the capture of Jerusalem by Titus, and it was adorned with a scene in which the soldiers of Titus may be seen bearing the spoils of the Temple, an altar and the seven-branched golden candlestick.

And because the Forum was not large enough for the increasing activities of Rome, one Forum after another was added. To commemorate his victory over the Dacians, which gave another province to the Empire, Trajan made the Forum in which there still stands the column with bas-reliefs portraying his campaigns. Such was its magnificence that when the Emperor Constantius beheld it after seeing the other glories of Rome, he remained speechless with admiration.

Surely the Roman had reason to be proud of his country! What had Christianity to offer worth his consideration as compared with her great achievements, with her far-stretching dominion? Christianity was perhaps regarded at first as a Jewish sect, for there must have been some considerable number of Jews in the Roman Church. In Rome the Jews were despised by educated society. Gallio's treatment of the Jews at Corinth would be typical of the attitude of many a Roman official. And how would the Roman regard the Christian message when the Christians confessed that the kingdom they sought was not of this world, that their citizenship was in Heaven? What a vague, unsubstantial dream to the practical Roman!

CHAPTER II

THE PLEASURES OF ROME

The Colosseum. The Baths of Caracalla and of Diocletian

IF the pride of Rome proved an obstacle to the advance of Christianity, the pleasures of Rome were perhaps no less a hindrance. Of these pleasures two kinds are vividly brought before us by the monuments they have left.

AMPHITHEATRES

The Colosseum was not built till fifteen years after the martyrdom of S. Paul. Battered and broken as are the remains which survive of the vast amphitheatre of the Flavian Emperors, yet their massive strength and stupendous size (for it could hold 90,000 spectators) impress the mind of the traveller with wonder and with horror as he reflects upon the purpose for which such buildings were made. The indifference with which the Roman regarded suffering, his callous recklessness in taking life, here receive their most signal example. At the dedication of the Colosseum by Titus 5,000 wild beasts were slaughtered in the arena. How pleasing such scenes of bloodshed were to the Roman world is shown by the vogue they attained in other cities of the Empire. He who would win popular favour knew that the way was to provide a spectacle in which men or beasts tore

THE PLEASURES OF ROME

one another in pieces. Trajan amused the people for 123 days by a spectacle of 10,000 captives engaged in mutual slaughter. Slaves were used for the same purpose. The number of slaves in Rome in the first century has been estimated as amounting to as much as half the population of the city. And though the lot of a slave under a good master was tolerable, in the hands of a brutal master he was exposed to the utmost atrocities. Not till the time of the Antonines did it become illegal to kill slaves or sell them for the amphitheatre.

To the victims of the amphitheatre were added the Christians. Whether it be true that in the Colosseum S. Ignatius suffered martyrdom, it is clear that it was to such a death that he looked forward whilst travelling under sentence of death from Antioch to Rome. For in the letter he sent to the Roman Church he writes:

I write to all the Churches, and I bid all men know, that of my own free will I die for God, unless ye should hinder me. . . . Let me be given to the wild beasts, for through them I can attain unto God. I am God's wheat, and I am ground by the teeth of wild beasts that I may be found pure bread [of Christ]. . . . Then shall I be truly a disciple of Jesus Christ, when the world shall not so much as see my body. Supplicate the Lord for me, that through these instruments I may be found a sacrifice to God. . . . Come fire and cross, and grapplings with wild beasts, wrenching of bones, hacking of limbs, crushings of my whole body. . . . Only be it mine to attain unto Jesus Christ. . . . Permit me to be an imitator of the passion of my God. . . . I write to you in the midst of life, yet lusting after death. My lust hath been crucified, and there is no fire of

EARLY CHRISTIANS OF ROME

material longing in me, but only water living and speaking in me, saying, Come to the Father.[1]

We may stand to-day in the Colosseum, and look around upon the vast array of seats from which once thousands of eager eyes were bent upon the spectacle of some little band of men and women as they were led into the arena to be given as a prey to the wild beasts. But for the martyrs it was the supreme hour of triumph, the victory of a faith which could meet and vanquish death.

Public Baths

The growing luxury of the Roman people in the days of the Empire is shown by the number and the magnificence of the public baths. Instituted at first for the poor, they became the resort of people of all classes. Of such establishments the huge Baths of Caracalla and of Diocletian are the most imposing monuments. The former is said to have been able to accommodate 1,600 persons at one time, the latter over 3,000. They contained not only baths of various kinds, cold, tepid, and hot, and rooms where the bathers were attended by slaves who rubbed and anointed them. They also included places of entertainment.

The Baths of Caracalla contained a library, a picture-gallery, a race-course, and a gymnasium. They were adorned with costly marble and mosaics, and with the finest works of art, of which some are still reckoned among the treasures of the civilized world to-day. And the

---

[1] Lightfoot, pp. 121 f.

THE PLEASURES OF ROME

meanest Roman, on payment of the smallest copper coin (or possibly indeed without payment), could procure, in the words of Gibbon—

> the daily enjoyment of a scene of pomp and luxury which might excite the envy of the kings of Asia. From these stately palaces issued a swarm of dirty and ragged plebeians ... who loitered away whole days in the street or forum, to hear news and to hold disputes; who dissipated, in extravagant gaming, the miserable pittance of their wives and children; and spent the hours of the night ... in the indulgence of gross and vulgar sensuality.[1]

Of those other more sordid forms of self-gratification this is not the place to speak. The Epistle to the Romans, chap. i., and the testimony of Roman writers are a sufficient commentary on the morals of the Roman world in the first century.

The conditions of life had undergone a profound change since the early days of Rome's history. Then devotion to duty, and the readiness to endure hardness and to submit to discipline, had been the foundation of the Roman character. To these Rome owed her greatness. But cheap entertainments and free doles of food given by the State formed one of the causes which kept in the capital a host of idlers and loafers to whom such an existence appeared preferable to the simple and strenuous life of the country-side. Thus the vigour of the Roman people was sapped, and they became no match for the hardier races of the North.

What was the task of Christianity in face of

[1] *Decline and Fall of the Roman Empire*, chap. xxxi.

these demoralizing conditions ? To rouse men by a trumpet-call, stern indeed in its demands, calling them to turn their back on things in which they had found their pleasure, and embrace a life of unremitting service, of daily discipline, of readiness for every sacrifice. It was to them that S. Paul wrote : " Now it is high time for you to awake out of sleep. . . . The night is far spent, the day is at hand ; let us therefore cast off the works of darkness, and let us put on the armour of light. Let us walk honestly, as in the day ; not in revelling and drunkenness, not in chambering and wantonness, not in strife and jealousy. But put ye on the Lord Jesus Christ, and make not provision for the flesh, to fulfil the lusts thereof." [1]

[1] Rom. xiii. 11 f.

CHAPTER III

THE RELIGIONS OF ROME

The Temples of Vesta, Jupiter Capitolinus, Portunus, Mater Matuta. The Mysteries: the Temple of Cybele: the Temples of Mithra. The Mysteries and Christianity

TEMPLES

THE primitive divinities of Rome were those of a simple agricultural people, Nature-spirits who had their dwelling in trees, in springs, on hill-tops, Jupiter, the sky-spirit, Saturnus, a spirit of agriculture, Mars, a spirit of agriculture and also of war. And there were the gods of the home, such as Janus, the god of the doorway, Vesta, goddess of the hearth-fire, and many others. No shrine was regarded with greater veneration than the little Temple of Vesta, where the sacred fire was kept ever burning, and of which the round base can still be seen in the Forum to-day.

As Rome extended her bounds, and her intercourse with neighbouring peoples increased, the divinities of these peoples came to take their place among the gods of Rome and to throw into the shade some of the primitive Nature-spirits, whilst some of the older divinities became merged in the new-comers. Thus the gods of Rome were identified with the gods of Olympus and assumed their functions whilst retaining their old names.

In 509 B.C. the great temple on the Capitol

EARLY CHRISTIANS OF ROME

was dedicated to the triad Jupiter, Juno, and Minerva. Two almost perfect temples standing by the Tiber recall the ancient divinities; the round temple probably dedicated to Portunus, the god of the harbour, and the beautiful temple close by commonly called the Temple of Fortuna Virilis, but more probably dedicated to Mater Matuta, the goddess of the dawn. This has happily been freed recently from the mean buildings which disfigured it, so that it now stands as it stood when rebuilt in the first century B.C.

The Graeco-Roman religion of the Republican Age became more and more a religion of the State. Cumont considers that there has perhaps never existed a religion so cold and so prosaic as that of the Romans, a religion subordinated to political aims, and seeking above all else by the strict performance of appropriate practices to secure for the State the protection of the gods or to avert the effects of their ill-will. Religion divorced from thought became a matter of unintelligible rites mechanically performed because they had been the custom of ancestors.[1] The old religious spirit grew ever feebler; the temples and festivals were neglected; and Varro, writing in the first century B.C., was afraid that the gods would perish, not by any hostile invasion, but by the neglect of the Roman citizens.

It was this that gave the mystery-religions their opportunity. By the first century A.D. Rome had become the meeting-place of mystery-

[1] *Les Religions orientales dans le paganisme romain*, pp. 44 ff. 1909.

THE RELIGIONS OF ROME

cults from Greece, from Egypt, from Asia Minor. The worship of Cybele, the Great Mother, was introduced into Rome in 204 B.C. The site of her temple on the Palatine is marked by the grove of ilexes standing on the mound in front of which there still is seated the headless figure of the goddess. Here every spring was re-enacted the drama of the death of Attis, the lover of Cybele, and his rising again, a festival celebrated with riotous orgies. The traveller sitting there alone while the wind whispers among the ilexes may yet seem to hear the din of flutes and drums and cymbals, and see the swaying crowd of frenzied and blood-stained votaries.

The cult of Isis and Serapis came from Egypt about 100 B.C. Isis was the goddess specially beloved by women. The story of her bereavement, her faithful search for the husband she had lost, and his return to life made her appear as the deity who could sympathize with those who love and suffer, and comfort them with the hope of life after death. She had numerous temples in Italy, one of which is still to be seen at Pompeii. Daily at dawn her shaven priests drew aside the white curtains before her shrine, and revealed the gorgeously-robed image of the goddess to her expectant worshippers, whilst sacrifices were offered and hymns resounded to the accompaniment of flutes.

These and other foreign mystery-cults appealed to those human instincts which the State religion had failed to satisfy—the emotions, the intelligence, and the conscience. They addressed themselves to the individual, not in his capacity of a Roman citizen, but as a human being, and

EARLY CHRISTIANS OF ROME

in their ranks no differences of race or class were recognized. Roman and Asiatic, master and slave, met in a common fellowship.

Moreover, they offered a satisfaction to some needs of the human spirit that were keenly felt in the Roman world of that time. They offered (*a*) a means of release from the wheel of Fate which men felt to press so hardly on human life; (*b*) purification from sin; (*c*) a way of attaining some knowledge of the Deity and entering into communion with Him; (*d*) the hope of immortality.

Unlike the gods of Olympus in their serene enjoyment of perpetual vigour were the gods of the mysteries, who suffered and died and lived again. If these cults were crude in their origin, springing from Nature-myths, the decay of vegetation at the approach of winter and its revival in the spring, if the legends of their deities contained elements of a gross and sensual character, if rites of a revolting kind were practised, yet they gained a host of votaries among the Roman people. The original barbarism lost some of its grossness by acquiring a more spiritual significance. Such seems to have been the case with the *taurobolium*, which was adopted by the worshippers of Cybele from the second century A.D. This consisted in the slaughter of a bull over a shallow pit, in which the candidate for initiation was placed to receive his baptism in the blood which poured down upon him. This savage rite, which was esteemed as having great efficacy, may have originated in the primitive idea that in this way the initiate could gain the

THE RELIGIONS OF ROME

vigour of the bull. But it came to be regarded as a new spiritual birth, and those who had undergone it believed themselves to have been "born again for eternity."

When Augustus rose to power, he made an attempt to revive the dying religion of ancient Rome, which he regarded as a useful instrument for maintaining political stability and good order. He claimed to have restored eighty-two temples, and built the temple to Mars the Avenger in his Forum which is now being opened up. Among his great works was a temple of extraordinary magnificence, dedicated to Apollo, on the Palatine close to his own palace.

The Pantheon (i.e. all-holy) was erected, as shown by the inscription over the portico, by his son-in-law Agrippa, but was almost entirely rebuilt under Hadrian. This stupendous temple, with its seven great niches for images of the gods, its colossal dome poised over the vast empty space beneath, and the one round aperture at its summit open to the sky through which alone the light enters the building, may serve as a fitting symbol of the Roman genius, its love of bigness, its austerity, and its massive strength.

The Romans possessed little artistic skill, and made free use of the work of Greek sculptors. The statues of the gods, which are among the chief glories of the galleries of Rome, present an embodiment of grace and beauty, of majesty, strength, and youthful vigour. The Roman moving among these splendours when they adorned his city might well hear with incredulous amazement of Romans who worshipped as their deity a Jew Who had suffered the hideous and ignominious penalty of crucifixion.

And the Christians who refused to pay the customary honour to the Emperor as if he were divine could hardly fail to appear disloyal to the majesty of the State which he represented.

But of all the forces opposed to Christianity from the end of the first century none perhaps was so formidable as the Persian mystery-cult of Mithra, which took root in Rome about that time and was carried by the Roman legions to the most remote provinces of the Empire. The monuments they have left are found from the Black Sea to the borders of Scotland and the frontiers of the Sahara. For Mithraism was a religion particularly attractive to soldiers. It encouraged the military virtues; it imposed severe self-discipline, abstinence, control of the passions. It imparted a sense of brotherhood. Mithra was not the supreme god in the Mithraic religion, but the mediator between the unapproachable and unknowable god who reigned in the ethereal spheres and the human race that struggled and suffered. Mithra had been compelled to catch a bull, and after a struggle to slay him. This is the scene which is met with again and again on the altars of Mithra. It was believed that from the body of the slaughtered bull all useful plants and useful animals were produced; whilst the dog, the scorpion, and other creatures in these pictures are the malevolent forces bent on destruction. Thus Mithra was presented to the eyes of his votaries as continually engaged in a struggle against the powers of evil. And it was Mithra who presided over

THE RELIGIONS OF ROME

the judgment of souls after death and guided their course upwards to the celestial mansions, where he received them like children returning from a long voyage.[1]

Mithra was the god of light, but his worship was carried on in underground temples such as that beneath the church of S. Clemente. It is a question whether the Mithraists adopted the *taurobolium*. Their cult appears to have been closely associated with the cult of Cybele, and the underground chapel in the Baths of Caracalla, which is said to be a temple of Mithra, has in the centre a shallow pit with a passage leading from it such as would have been required for the *taurobolium*. The sacrifice of a bull took place on certain great occasions. At other times birds were offered.

Those who desired to be initiated into the mysteries of Mithra were required to go through a long and painful course of preparation. An oath was exacted called *sacramentum*; repeated lustrations were prescribed to wash away the stains of guilt, and for this purpose a fount was provided in the temple. At a certain stage the initiate was allowed to partake in a sacred rite in which a loaf and a cup of wine and water were placed before the priest, who pronounced over it a sacred formula. By partaking of this mystical food the neophyte was believed to gain power to combat malignant spirits, or even to gain immortality.

Sunday was considered a day specially holy as being the day sacred to the sun, and special prayers were provided. The great festival was

[1] Cumont, *Mysteries of Mithra*, p. 145.

held on December 25, the birthday of " the unconquerable sun," when the days begin to lengthen.

It was in the third century that Mithraism rose to the zenith of its power. Can we wonder that Christian Apologists should see in its rites the device of devils to imitate and rival the Christian religion?[1] Yet the mystery-religions, for all the gross and crude naturalism which disfigured them, had recognized the yearning desires and needs of the human mind and conscience, and had attempted, however imperfectly, to provide that for which the world was waiting, a way of redemption. But they passed out of existence, and Christianity lives on to this day. What enabled it to come victorious out of the conflict with Mithraism? In part because of a weakness in the Mithraic system which did not admit women to its fellowship.

And between Christianity and all the mystery-cults there was a difference which was fundamental. The mystery-religions were founded on myths of legendary figures who had no real existence; but Christianity on One Who had lived on earth a human life, a man among men, and Who was yet God incarnate, the Saviour of mankind, Who had died to redeem the world.

Against the power of that Faith Paganism in all its forms strove in vain. The followers of Christ, crucified and thrown to wild beasts, set up as living torches in the pleasure-grounds of Nero and sent to perish in the mines, were possessed of an indestructible life. Is there any

[1] As Justin, about A.D. 152, *Apol.* i. 66.

S. PETER.
IN *SS. PIETRO E MARCELLINO.*
3RD CENTURY.

facing p. 20.

THE RELIGIONS OF ROME

place, at any rate in the Western world, which
can bring in the same measure as Rome so vivid
a sense of the reality of the Communion of
Saints, of oneness with those who have gone
before, of the littleness of death?

For the saints live on. Their labours have
endured and will endure. Their presence is still
living and powerful to-day. Since the first
century nations have come and gone. States
have fallen and disappeared. Crumbling ruins
are all that is left of the palaces of the Cæsars.
What remains of the tomb of the great Augustus
is now used by the Romans as a concert-hall.
In the centre of the mighty mausoleum which
Hadrian built for himself, and in which he and
the Antonine Emperors found their last resting-
place, the lofty hall which once contained their
tombs is empty. The porphyry which covered
the ashes of Hadrian is said by some to be
what is now used as the font in the baptistery
of S. Peter's. But in the great churches which
rise above the tombs of S. Paul and S. Peter
the saints are still honoured by multitudes who
know nothing of the most illustrious names of
Rome. Thousands come from distant lands to
visit the city where they laboured and suffered,
and the places where their bodies were laid.
And to many thousands more, even to the ends
of the earth, their labours and sufferings are
known and had in reverence. Their very words,
in the tongues of many races, have become a
familiar possession. True it is that "their
sound is gone out into all lands, and their
words into the ends of the world."

CHAPTER IV

EARLY CHRISTIAN ROME

Jewish and Christian Catacombs

WE have seen how the faith of the early Christians was proved to possess a power more irresistible, more enduring, than the apparently impregnable might of pagan Rome, a power that enabled them to triumph over sufferings and over death in its most fearful forms. What was this faith?

The answer to this question is to be found not only in the teaching of the leaders of the Church. The victory was won, not by their heroism alone, but by the faith of the undistinguished multitude of the faithful.

In the very ancient Church of S. Maria Antiqua beneath the Palatine there are frescoes of many renowned saints with their names. There is also a little group of unnamed saints with the inscription: " Whose names the Lord knoweth." They may stand for the host of those who lived in the faith of Christ and may have suffered for His sake, but of whom no record remains on earth. Of such were those whom we are now to consider.

In the inscriptions and pictures on countless Christian tombs these unknown saints speak to us in their own words, and put before us in their own way their thoughts and hopes and beliefs

EARLY CHRISTIAN ROME

about God, about the redemption wrought by Christ, and the Communion of Saints, and the Sacraments, and the life beyond death.

Much indeed has perished irretrievably. Inscriptions and paintings have faded or disappeared; some can only now be seen in the copies made by travellers of past generations. But in the Catacombs and churches and museums of Rome much of those past ages still lives before the eyes which know how to discern its meaning.

Remains of pagan tombs and sarcophagi (stone coffins) also abound in and around Rome. Burial was not allowed within the walls of the city, and the tombs were erected along the roads beyond the city gates. Their ruins rise for miles beside the Appian Way, and are still visible on the Via Latina ere it loses itself in the Campagna.

The epitaphs show that certain conventional forms were in use. At the head: D.M., or DIS MANIBUS, i.e. "to the spirits of the world of the dead." Then follow the name and age of the departed, and sometimes words expressing affection, or praise of his good qualities added by the relative or friend who states that the tomb was erected by him. The sarcophagus was frequently decorated with carvings representing the deceased, or scenes derived from mythology, or the legends of heroes, scenes of warfare, the hunting of wild beasts, agricultural pursuits, nymphs, or sea-horses. The funeral chamber containing the tombs was sometimes adorned with paintings or stucco-work representing figures, birds, and foliage.

EARLY CHRISTIANS OF ROME

The Catacombs

Very different from the wayside tombs of pagan Rome were the burial-places of the Jews and of the Christians in the first three centuries A.D. Around the city the soil is honeycombed with passages extending for many miles, and only partially explored, so that their full extent cannot be precisely known. In the walls of these underground passages horizontal niches have been hewn out of the soil to receive the bodies. The niches when occupied were closed in with a slab of stone or marble on which the epitaph was graven. It seems that when there remained no more space for burial, a second passage was dug out below the first, and later perhaps a third below the second, and others even lower still.

The number and size of the Jewish Catacombs witness to the extent of the Jewish community in Rome.

The Jewish inscriptions are for the most part in Greek, some in Latin; Hebrew inscriptions other than a single word—*Shalom*, i.e. peace—are rare. The words in Greek, "May his [*or*, her] sleep be in peace," are found again and again. But the Jewish origin of these inscriptions is made sufficiently clear by the various symbolic figures which frequently accompany them. Of these by far the commonest is a representation of the seven-branched candlestick brought to Rome among the spoils of the Temple. It has been suggested that the significance of the candlestick on tombs may be explained by the words in the Greek Bible: " The spirit of man is the light of the Lord " (Prov. xx. 27).

EARLY CHRISTIAN ROME

Other signs are a palm-branch, a dove and a curved object thought to represent the Shofar, i.e. the sacred trumpet made of a ram's horn which was blown at the Feast of Tabernacles and was intended to symbolize the resurrection of the dead which should precede the Messianic times to be announced by the Shofar.[1]

The palm-branch on Jewish tombs is sometimes found together with what is thought to represent a citron. In the processions which took place at the Feast of Tabernacles the worshippers carried in one hand a citron, and in the other the "lulab," i.e. a palm-branch with sprigs of myrtle and willow fastened to the lower end. This was in accordance with the precept of Lev. xxiii. 40, the citron being held to be "the fruit of the goodly tree."

The Feast of Tabernacles was *par excellence* "the season of our joy."[2] Is the use of these figures on graves due to an expectation that the future life will be a continual feast of rejoicing such as the joy of Tabernacles? Indications of such a belief may be found in 2 Esdras ii. 11, and S. Mark ix. 5, and would explain the significance of S. Peter's proposal. It was due to his conviction that the kingdom of God had indeed come. Such a belief may also explain our Lord's use of the expression "eternal tabernacles" for the abode into which the faithful will be received hereafter.[3]

In later times, at any rate, it was customary on the Sabbath before the eighth day of the

---

[1] *Jewish Encyclopædia*, vol. iii, p. 616.
[2] E.g. *Book of Jubilees*, xvi. 13–31.
[3] S. Luke xvi. 9.

Feast to make mention in the prayers of departed relations and friends, and to make charitable offerings for the repose of their souls.[1]

The Christian tombs have a richness, a variety, and a character all their own. Yet it is natural that in the earliest days of the Roman Church they should show some traces of the influence of Jewish and even of pagan sepulchral conventions. If a Christian wished to purchase a carved sarcophagus, he might have to resort to a pagan craftsman, but he would naturally choose from among the sarcophagi he found in stock one which would least conflict with his ideas as a Christian. Thus, scenes of agricultural life might be accepted, but not figures of heathen divinities unless in some way they could be brought into accord with Christian ideas. A representation of a shepherd could thus come for the Christian to represent the Good Shepherd, and in the absence of any distinctive Christian signs it is not always possible to pronounce with certainty as to the pagan or the Christian origin of such figures. Professor Marucchi is of opinion that there are few sarcophagi of Christian origin of an earlier date than the Peace of Constantine (early in the fourth century), but that even in the third century some attempts were made to sculpture the favourite subjects, viz. the Good Shepherd, the Orante (i.e. the soul in prayer), and the anchor.[2]

[1] A. W. Greenup, *Sukkah, Mishna and Tosefta*, p. 24.
[2] *Éléments d'archéologie chrétienne*, i. p. 262.

CHAPTER V

CHRISTIAN SEPULCHRAL INSCRIPTIONS

FOR the earliest Christian art we must go to the Catacombs, of which some (S. Priscilla and S. Domitilla) belong to the first century. Here by the light of flickering tapers we can discern the figures traced by the hands of our fellow-Christians eighteen centuries ago, and we can read the words in which they expressed their faith with regard to their blessed dead. These inscriptions are sometimes a curious mixture of Greek and Latin, with words frequently misspelt, and showing little regard for grammatical accuracy. But it is just these linguistic defects which make them of special value for our purpose.

The words " IN PACE " (in peace) are characteristic of Christian burial. These two simple words, either by themselves or with other words, are found on innumerable graves. If they owed something to the Jewish tradition we have noticed above, the Christians filled them with a new meaning. Death, so far as it could be regarded as a sleep, was only the sleep of the body in the tomb. For the soul, IN PEACE means not sleep but life, life eternal, life in Christ, life in the fellowship of the saints, a life of prayer, a life mindful of those who had been loved on earth and of their needs.

EARLY CHRISTIANS OF ROME

The following are typical examples of many others in the Catacombs:

Victorina, in peace and in Christ.

Baccis, sweet soul, in the peace of the Lord. She lived 15 years, a virgin. (S. Callixtus.)

Julia in peace with the saints.

Others are as follows:

The Lord is with thee. (S. Priscilla.)

O Bettonius, in peace. May God be with thy spirit. ICHTHUS.[1] (S. Callixtus.)

To his most sweet brother. He rests in peace with God in peace.

Aur. Agapetilla, the handmaid of God, who sleeps in peace; she lived 21 years 3 months and 4 days. Her father made this [tomb].

Prima, thou livest in the glory of God and in the peace of our Lord Christ.

Thou wilt live in God. (Lateran Museum.)

Mayest thou live in God. (Lateran Museum.)

Mayest thou live in the Lord Jesus. (Lateran Museum.)

Mayest thou live in the Holy Spirit. (S. Callixtus.)

Secundianus [who believed in] Christ Jesus lives [or, may he live] in the Father and in the Holy Spirit. (S. Domitilla.)

O Hermaiscus thou light, thou livest in the Lord God Christ. 10 years and 7 months. (Lateran Museum.)

Thou wilt live for ever. (Lateran Museum.)

On the tomb of a beloved brother:

Theodorus, we live in God [a drawing of a fish]. (S. Priscilla.)

[1] See p. 47.

SEPULCHRAL INSCRIPTIONS

May thy spirit [dwell] among the saints. (S. Callixtus.)

The body of Julia Evarista, most dear to God, lies here, and her soul being renewed by the Spirit of Christ, and having received an angelic body, she was taken up to the heavenly kingdom of Christ with the saints.

May God give thee light.

Believing in Christ he has the recompense of light.

Timothea, eternal light be thine in Christ. She lived 13 years 9 months. In peace.

An inscription once in the Catacomb of S. Priscilla but now lost:

Maritima, thou reverend one, thou didst not leave the pleasant light behind thee, for thou hadst with thee [a drawing of a fish and an anchor] Him Who is immortal in all things, for thy piety has gone before thee everywhere.

Anicius Petronius Probus, a man of illustrious descent, held high offices of State in the latter part of the fourth century. His sarcophagus, now in the Museo Petriano, bore an inscription which, after mentioning the honours that he had enjoyed during his lifetime, continued:

Now art thou nearer to Christ, and hast gained the abode of the Saints: thine is the joy of new light, for Christ thy light is with thee.

Some inscriptions speak of the life beyond as *refrigerium*, i.e. refreshment.

May God refresh thy spirit. (Lateran Museum.)

May thy spirit be refreshed in good. (S. Domitilla.)

Sweet Privata, be refreshed and in peace. (S. Priscilla.)

The noun and the corresponding verb *refrigero*

seem in common parlance to denote the refreshment which comes from rest, or food, or drink, and are applied in a spiritual sense to the refreshment of the soul when it finds its full satisfaction in God. The word *refrigerium* thus occurs frequently in the ancient Liturgies in prayers for the departed, as, e.g., in the Gregorian Sacramentary:

Remember, O Lord, Thy servants who have gone before us with the sign of faith, and rest in the sleep of peace. To them, O Lord, and to all who rest in Christ, grant a place of refreshment, of light, and peace, we beseech Thee.[1]

Again, in the *Missale Gothicum* (end of seventh century):

By the intercession of Thy holy martyrs grant, O Lord, to our beloved who sleep in Christ, refreshment in the land of the living.[2]

Peace, light, refreshment: these then all down the ages the Church has asked for her children departed. Such prayers are a constant feature of the ancient Liturgies.

Here are some epitaphs inscribed on the tombs of children:

Maurentius to Maurentia who lived 5 years 11 months and 2 days. God bade her to come into the company of the saints for which she was meet. In peace.

Severa, dear to her parents and servants, a virgin, rendered up [her soul] . . . which the Lord in His wondrous wisdom and knowledge had commanded [to come] into the flesh; which body tranquil in peace is buried here until it rise again through Him Who by His Holy Spirit has taken

[1] *P.L.* lxxviii. col. 28.   [2] *P.L.* lxxii. col. 308.

SEPULCHRAL INSCRIPTIONS

her soul always chaste, and modest, and inviolable, which the Lord will give back again in spiritual glory. She lived 9 years and 11 months and 15 days. Thus was she taken out of this world. (S. Callixtus.)

[Euse]bius, little child, by reason of his age without sin, having entered into the abode of the saints, rests in peace. (Found in Cemetery of Commodilla.)

Cyriacus lived 3 years 10 months and 5 days. His soul for ever with the saints in the name of Jesus Christ.

To Paul, my son, in peace. May the spirits of all the saints receive thee. He lived two years. (From Rome. Now at Carseoli.)

Let there be no sad tears, no beating upon your breast, O father and mother, for I have reached the heavenly realms. Gloomy Erebus doth not hold me, nor the pallid form of death, but serene rest; and sportive dances among blessed spirits and the pleasures of the good, all these things which grace Evodia doth Christ bestow. (S. Agnese.)

Laurentius, innocent soul, a lamb without spot, who departed from this world. He lived 15 years 5 months 3 days.

Some inscriptions contain a prayer addressed to God for the departed :

Lord, Who callest all to Thyself, receive the soul of Bonifatius for Thy holy Name's sake. (S. Callixtus.)

O God, Who sittest at the right hand of the Father, write the soul of Nectarius in the abode of Thy saints.

Father of all, Thou didst create Irene, Zoe, and Marcellus, receive [*or*, Thou didst also receive] them unto Thyself : to Thee be glory in Christ. (S. Priscilla.)

EARLY CHRISTIANS OF ROME

Demetris and Leontia to their daughter Sirica. Jesu, be mindful of our child. (S. Domitilla.)

Another prays the brethren that whenever they come to pray at the tomb of " dear Agape " they would make request for her in all their prayers to the Father and the Son, that God Almighty would keep her to all eternity. (S. Priscilla.)

The tomb of Lucifera bears the petition that any of the brethren who should read it may pray to God to receive unto Himself her holy and innocent spirit. (Lateran Museum.)

In the following the prayers of the departed are requested:

In thy prayers pray for us, for we know that thou [dwellest] in Christ. (Lateran Museum.)

Live, and may Jesus [keep] thy soul in peace, and pray for us. (S. Callixtus.)

On the tomb of a child aged seven:

May thy spirit [drawing of a dove] rest well in God [drawing of a fish]: pray for thy sister. (Lateran Museum.)

Dionysius, a child without guile, lies here. With the saints. Remember us also in your holy prayers, and him who carved and inscribed this.

Atticus, sleep in peace, safe beyond all harm, and pray earnestly for our sins. (Capitoline Museum.)

In this inscription it is clear that *sleep* does not signify unconsciousness.

About two miles outside the city, on the Appian Way, is the Basilica of S. Sebastiano with Catacombs beneath. This place has from very early days been associated in a peculiar way with the Apostles S. Paul and S. Peter.

SEPULCHRAL INSCRIPTIONS

An inscription placed there by Pope Damasus (fourth century) states that at one time they dwelt there. The meaning of this has been much disputed; some think that it refers to the residence of S. Peter in the neighbourhood, his name being coupled, as usual in early days, with that of S. Paul. But according to other scholars it refers to a temporary abode in this place of the bodies of the two Apostles, a date soon after the middle of the third century being suggested, the bodies being at some subsequent time restored to the localities in which they had previously rested, i.e. the site of S. Paul without the walls, and the Vatican Hill. Here have been found a large number of fragments with inscriptions which had been scratched upon the walls, apparently by those who came to pay honour to the Apostles, whether it were that their bodies were actually resting there at the time, or whether they had become closely associated with this place in the memory of the early Christians.

Most of the inscriptions are in Latin, but some in Greek, and the largest number consist of such invocations as the following:

Paul and Peter, pray for Victor.

Paul and Peter, pray for Eratus and ask . . .

Paul and Peter, keep in mind Sozomenus and . . .

Paul and Peter, pray for Nativus for ever.

Another asks that Peter and Paul would keep in mind Primus and members of his family, that they may live eternally in Christ.

CHAPTER VI

EARLY CHRISTIAN PICTURES ON SEPULCHRAL MONUMENTS

Their interpretation

WE must now see what further light is thrown upon the faith of the early Christians of Rome by the drawings and paintings in the Catacombs and, later, by the carvings on the sarcophagi. Certain signs and figures can be shown to be characteristic of the earlier age, whilst others are not found till the fuller development of Christian art which took place in the fourth century.

We notice a reserve in depicting the objects of their faith, particularly in the earlier days, when Christians were a hated and persecuted sect. Accordingly, signs and figures were employed which, while well understood by the faithful, would convey little to the world outside, if any from outside should chance to see them. When Christianity became the religion of the Government the caution and concealment hitherto necessary could be abandoned. The Christian faith could emerge from the Catacombs into the full light of day, and be freely represented in the manner shown by the beautiful and elaborate figures carved on the sarcophagi, and by the paintings and mosaics in the churches.

When we seek to interpret these representations, whether the earlier pictures in the Catacombs or the later sculptures, we are met with the difficulty that in most cases they are left to speak for themselves without any words of explanation. Are we to assume that they have a symbolical meaning ? In the case of some it would be generally agreed that the object represented is a symbol expressing certain religious conceptions. Such are the fish and the anchor. But in the case of others it may be asked if we are justified in seeking any significance beyond the obvious one presented, e.g. when Christ appears as changing the water into wine, or giving sight to the blind.

Certainly it would be possible, by giving the rein to one's fancy, to find meanings which were very far from the minds of those by whom these things were produced. These people are not to be thought of as setting out to " produce a theological system in pictures," and we must be on our guard against the attempt to read into their productions the ideas belonging to a later age, and to prove from them beliefs which did not come within the horizon of the early Church. We must seek to look at these things with the eyes which beheld them in the second or third century.

Therefore we must notice in the first place the extensive use made of symbolism in the early Church as a means of expressing Christian truths. We have examples in the New Testament itself. The Epistle to the Hebrews, now commonly regarded as addressed most probably to a circle of Christians living in Rome, has made large use of this method in interpreting the events of the Old Testament. Again, the Fourth

EARLY CHRISTIANS OF ROME

Evangelist has written in order to give a spiritual interpretation of the events of the Gospel history. He relates the feeding of the multitude, and then goes on to explain that it symbolizes the feeding of the hungry multitudes throughout the world with the Bread of life. He relates the giving of sight to the blind man, and sets forth the teaching of Christ as the Light of the world.

The same use of symbolism appears in the early Christian hymn-book known as *The Odes of Solomon*, which shows some marked resemblances to the Fourth Gospel.

In the Christian department of the Lateran Museum there is a part of a monument from the tomb of Abercius, Bishop of Hieropolis in Phrygia, in which he recounts the journey he made from Nisibis to Rome, about A.D. 170. Some of the imagery he employs will meet us again in the monuments of Rome. It is as follows :

The citizen of a notable city I made this [tomb] in my lifetime ; that in due season I might have here a resting-place for my body. Abercius by name, I am a disciple of the pure Shepherd, Who feedeth His flocks of sheep on mountains and plains, Who hath great eyes looking on all sides ; for He taught me faithful writings. He also sent me to royal Rome to behold it and to see the golden-robed, golden-slippered Queen. And there I saw a people bearing the splendid seal. And I saw the plain of Syria and all the cities, even Nisibis, crossing over the Euphrates. And everywhere I had associates. In company with Paul, I followed, while everywhere Faith led the way, and set before me for food the fish from the fountain, mighty and stainless (whom a pure virgin grasped), and gave this to friends to eat always, having good wine and giving the mixed cup with bread.[1]

Here Abercius describes in figurative language how he, a disciple of Christ, found Christians in Rome and in all the places through which he passed (associates), and everywhere the same faith (that taught by S. Paul), and everywhere the same Sacraments, *the seal* being the name given in the early Church to Baptism and Confirmation, and *the fish* meaning Christ, the spiritual food given in the Eucharistic Bread and the mixed Chalice to those who are friends in the unity of the Church.

Another example is to be found in the hymn attributed to S. Clement of Alexandria about A.D. 200.[2] Here he addresses Christ as:

The Shepherd of royal lambs, the Helm, the Bridle, the heavenly Wing of the all-holy flock, the Fisher of men who are being saved, enticing chaste fishes with sweet life from the hateful wave of a sea of vices.

The writings of other early Fathers supply abundant evidence of the practice of attaching figurative meanings to the stories both of the Old and of the New Testaments. It has been said that the early Christians were more concerned to represent truths than mere events, not external facts but their spiritual significance. An examination of these early Christian monuments may bear out this conclusion. We do not observe that the attempt is made to portray their subjects with literal accuracy.

We notice that certain subjects are repeated

[1] Translation in Kidd, *Documents*, vol. i, p. 111.
[2] *P.G.* viii. col. 681.

EARLY CHRISTIANS OF ROME

again and again in the paintings of the Catacombs and on the sarcophagi, and eventually in a manner that has become conventional. These, we may reasonably assume, are those which occupied a foremost place in the minds of those who put them there. These are the subjects on which, as we see, they preferred to dwell in the face of death. Why are these particular subjects chosen? And there are other subjects which to us might seem equally striking or suitable, but which do not appear at all.

In seeking an explanation we are not left entirely to conjecture. Certain clues are available which throw light both on the choice of subjects and on their interpretation.

1. Some of the signs reflect the ideas of the ancient world, and when adopted and adapted by the Christians they may yet retain something of their original meaning, e.g. the dolphin.

2. It was necessary to choose subjects which could be easily recognized by some characteristic feature, e.g. the man carrying his bed.

3. It is clear that certain subjects would make a specially forcible appeal to Christians living under the conditions prevailing in Rome during the first three centuries. The stories of Daniel among the lions and of the three young men in the fiery furnace would naturally impress in a peculiar way the imaginations of those who lived under the constant menace of persecution, and who knew that they themselves were liable to be thrown to the lions, and who had before their minds such scenes as those in the pleasure-grounds of Nero described by Tacitus.[1] The

[1] *Annals*, xv. 44. See Appendix.

PICTURES ON SEPULCHRAL MONUMENTS

choice of subjects such as these would be sufficiently accounted for without seeking any further theological significance. And this applies particularly to the earlier days.

4. We know that in the seventh century in Rome candidates for Baptism were assembled in church on Easter Eve before proceeding to the baptistery of the Lateran, where the rites of Baptism took place. Passages of Scripture were read aloud.

The lections chosen for the occasion were meant to present a summary of the relations between man and God, and to form, as it were, a final instruction at the moment of the accomplishment of the mystery of initiation. These lections are practically the same in all the Latin rituals. Some of the finest passages in the Old Testament are presented in them.[1]

They included the accounts of the Creation, the Deluge, the sacrifice of Isaac, Jonah, and the image set up by Nebuchadnezzar, narratives which we see portrayed on the monuments. If this represents the custom of the earlier centuries, then these subjects and the interpretation given to them would come to be for those who heard them woven into the fabric of their Christian belief.

5. A clue to the interpretation of a particular fresco is sometimes suggested by other frescoes around it, pointing to a connexion of ideas.

6. The representations which we are considering belong to sepulchral monuments. We cannot suppose that they were chosen at

[1] Duchesne, p. 308.

EARLY CHRISTIANS OF ROME

haphazard, but rather that they were deliberately chosen because they expressed certain beliefs concerning death and the life beyond. When we find references to the same subjects in the writings of the early Fathers, particularly those of the Western Church, and in the early Liturgies, and there also in connexion with the departed, we have good evidence that certain ideas were then current according to which a particular significance was attached to these subjects. But as we shall see, the same subject might be interpreted in a variety of ways; and it does not follow that because it is interpreted in a particular way by a writer in Carthage or Gaul, or in a Liturgy of the seventh or eighth century, such an application must necessarily have been in the mind of the Christian living in Rome in the second or third century. Such an assumption would be quite unwarranted.

Yet it must be borne in mind that to Rome, the meeting-place of people from all lands, the ideas current in one part of the Church were most likely to find their way, even if those ideas had not arisen in Rome itself. The inscription of Abercius quoted above (p. 36) is evidence of the community of thought throughout the Church in the second century.

The history of the Roman Liturgy is very obscure. The early Church of Rome was Greek-speaking, and the original Liturgy was in Greek. During the fourth century this seems to have given place to a Latin Liturgy. The Roman Service-books which have come down to us are not earlier than the sixth century. The Leonian Sacramentary is considered to

PICTURES ON SEPULCHRAL MONUMENTS

belong to the sixth century, the Gelasian Sacramentary to the seventh century, and the Gregorian Sacramentary to the eighth century. The two last appear to contain some elements of non-Roman origin, but it will be generally admitted that ecclesiastical usage tends to be conservative, and the history of liturgical development shows that the Church of Rome was slow to make any changes. When therefore we find a practice, such as that of the commemoration of the faithful departed, in the Liturgies of the West as well as of the East, we have good reason for believing that it was no innovation introduced into the Roman Liturgy for the first time in the seventh or eighth century.

Dom Leclercq considers that the choice of the Old Testament subjects may be explained by the influence of the Liturgies. " Les prières liturgiques les plus anciennes, dont les invocations trouvent dans les fresques leur commentaire perpétuel." [1]

Professor Marucchi goes so far as to say that early Christian art is unintelligible unless compared with the Liturgies.[2]

At the second Council of Nicæa (A.D. 787) it was declared that the manner of representing sacred subjects was regulated by the established sanction and tradition of the Catholic Church.[3]

It need perhaps hardly be said that this attempt to see what light is thrown upon the

[1] *Dict. d'arch. chrét. et de lit.*, vol. ii, col. 2476.
[2] *Éléments d'arch. chrét.*, i. p. 264.
[3] Labbe, *Concil.*, vol. vii, p. 831.

EARLY CHRISTIANS OF ROME

early monuments of Rome by the Christian thought and practice of the time makes no pretension to be anything more than a very brief and partial view of what would be a vast field of study. It must suffice to give some examples which, it is hoped, may prove suggestive; and should this be successful in lighting up, if only with a few faint gleams, the life of those distant ages, that is all that this little book can hope to accomplish.

Some of the interpretations given by early writers may indeed seem to a modern mind fanciful and far-fetched. But that does not make them of less value for our purpose, which is to gain some insight into the minds of the Christians of the early centuries.

CHAPTER VII

CHRISTIAN SYMBOLS

Symbols of Christ: the Good Shepherd, Orpheus, the Fish, the Dolphin. Meaning of the Orante.

OUR consideration of the monuments will naturally begin with the various forms in which our Lord is represented, both because His is the central Figure, and because it appears among the earliest paintings in the Catacombs.

The sign ☧, being the first letters of the name Christ, is hardly to be found before the time of Constantine, i.e. when standing by itself, and not merely as an abbreviation in the text of an inscription, though the form ✶ may be earlier.

The form ☧ again is later.

The halo is of pagan origin, but was adopted by the Christians and at first reserved for figures of Christ and the angels. In the fifth century it is found also on figures of the Blessed Virgin and the saints.

THE GOOD SHEPHERD

This is found as early as the first century in the Catacomb of S. Domitilla, and continually during the following centuries. The Good Shepherd is represented as youthful and beardless during the first two or three centuries. He stands bearing the lamb on His shoulder,

EARLY CHRISTIANS OF ROME

sometimes with the equipment of the shepherd, the pastoral flute, the staff, and the milk-pail. Afterwards He appears also in the midst of a flock of sheep, and sometimes with other figures, such as the Apostles, around Him.

Eusebius relates that the Emperor Constantine put up on the fountains at Constantinople figures of the Good Shepherd " well known to those who study the sacred oracles." [1]

It is clear from the very frequent occurrence of representations of the Good Shepherd at Rome that it was in this aspect above all others that the early Roman Christians loved to picture our Lord.

And if it was to Christians in Rome that the Epistle to the Hebrews was addressed, the writer was in that case making use of a name which he knew would make a special appeal to his readers : " The God of peace Who brought again from the dead the great Shepherd of the sheep." [2]

The Shepherd Who had laid down His life for His sheep and had been brought again from the dead might well seem a fitting picture to place over the tombs of the faithful departed. In the New Testament the title is used, outside the Gospels, in this passage and 1 Peter only, ii. 25, v. 4. And that 1 Peter was written from Rome is held to be very probable.

S. Clement, writing from Rome at the close of the first century, calls the Church " the flock of Christ." [3]

Abercius, as we have seen (p. 36), received his mission to Rome from " the pure Shepherd

[1] *Vita Constantini*, iii. 49 ; *P.G.* xx. col. 1109.
[2] xiii. 20.   [3] Lightfoot, pp. 34, 35.

CHRIST AS THE GOOD SHEPHERD.
IN *THE CHRISTIAN MUSEUM OF THE LATERAN.*

facing p. 44.

CHRISTIAN SYMBOLS

Who feedeth His flocks on mountains and plains."

In the hymn of S. Clement of Alexandria (p. 37) Christ is thrice addressed as "the Shepherd."

Occasionally the shepherd is represented in the act of milking his sheep. There is an allusion to such an idea in *The Passion of S. Perpetua*. She suffered martyrdom in North Africa about A.D. 203. She relates that in a vision which she had before her death she seemed to mount a ladder which reached to Heaven, and came to a large garden in the midst of which a man was seated, white-haired, in the dress of a shepherd, and engaged in milking his sheep. Around him stood many thousands arrayed in white. And he said, "Welcome, my child," and he gave her as it were a mouthful of curdled milk, which she received in her hands placed together and ate, and all who stood around said, Amen. At the sound of their voices she awoke, and knew that it portended that she would suffer martyrdom.[1]

S. Perpetua has been regarded with peculiar veneration in the Church of Rome, her name having a place among the saints who are commemorated in the Canon of the Mass.

Tertullian draws from the parable of the lost sheep an argument for the resurrection of the body. Our Lord says that He is come to save that which is lost. What is lost ? The whole of man, his body as well as his soul. Hence :

Since it is the bodily substance as well as the soul, making up the entire animal, which was

[1] *P.L.* iii. cols. 25–29.

borne on the shoulders of the Good Shepherd, we have here unquestionably an example how man is restored in both his natures.

Otherwise he would only be saved in part, and that would show that God has not the power to relieve and help him in his entire state.[1]

The Office of the Dead in the Gelasian Sacramentary contains a prayer to " God to Whom all things live " that He would grant to the soul of the deceased to be borne upon the shoulders of the Good Shepherd and brought to the flock of the saints and the faithful in great light, in the land, in the realm of the living.[2]

Orpheus

In several pictures, of which the earliest belongs to the second century, a figure appears which is commonly held to represent Christ in the guise of Orpheus, with his lyre. In one which has now perished, He was shown sitting on a mountain with birds, lions and other beasts around Him, captivated by the music. (S. Domitilla. Third century.)

Eusebius says that the Grecian myth tells that Orpheus had power to charm ferocious beasts and tame their savage spirit by striking the chords of his lyre, and by its power even the trees were moved from their places. But the all-wise Word of God, desiring to heal the manifold diseases of the souls of men, used that human nature which is the workmanship of His own wisdom, as an instrument by the melodious strains of which He soothed, not brute beasts,

[1] *De Resur. Carnis*, 34, about A.D. 209 ; *P.L.* ii. col. 842.
[2] *P.L.* lxxiv. col. 1234.

but savages endued with reason, healing each fierce and angry passion, both of civilized and barbarous people, by the medicine of His divine teaching.[1]

In other frescoes Orpheus appears with sheep, not wild beasts, around him (e.g. S. Callixtus).

It may be a matter for surprise that Christians should have made use of a heathen myth to represent the work of Christ. And S. Clement of Alexandria expresses his disapproval, contrasting the Orpheus of the Greek myth with Christ, by Whose music men are tamed, but also freed and uplifted.[2]

It has indeed been questioned whether the early Christian artists had any intention of making a representation of Christ when painting the figure of Orpheus, or whether they merely made use of an idyllic scene for the purpose of decoration. Yet the words of S. Clement may imply that he was aware that the figure of Orpheus had been used to represent our Lord, nor is it so surprising that this should have been done if we reflect that early Christian art had only succeeded in partially emancipating itself from the influence of classical traditions, and only gradually evolved an art entirely Christian.

THE FISH. IN GREEK, $IX\Theta Y\Sigma$

This figure occurs very frequently, and was used to express very various conceptions.

It is the most ancient symbol of Christ, and was extensively employed during the first three centuries when the Christians felt the necessity

---

[1] *P.G.* xx. col. 1409.   [2] *P.G.* viii. col. 55.

EARLY CHRISTIANS OF ROME

of observing caution in representing the subjects of their faith. After A.D. 313 this symbol disappears. The Greek word is composed of

THE EUCHARISTIC FISH IN THE CRYPT OF LUCINA.

the initial letters of JESUS CHRIST: SON OF GOD: SAVIOUR. This is the explanation given by S. Augustine.[1] The use of this figure, therefore, was a confession of faith in the sacred mission and Divine Sonship of our Lord and in His work of Redemption.

S. Augustine, in the passage above mentioned, gives a further explanation:

By the name FISH, Christ is to be understood, because He was able to live, that is, without sin, in the abyss of our mortality as if in the depth of the waters.

The symbol is further accounted for by four stories in the Gospels, viz. the feeding of the five thousand and the feeding of the four thousand with loaves and fishes, the repast of bread and fish of which the disciples partook at the Sea of Tiberias (S. John xxi.), and the finding of the stater in the fish's mouth. For the three first of these see under EUCHARIST, pp. 100 ff. The fourth story is interpreted by S. Jerome as

[1] *De Civit. Dei*, xviii. 23; *P.L.* xli. col. 580.

CHRISTIAN SYMBOLS

signifying the price paid by Christ to save sinners.[1]

Another meaning of the symbol is given by the author of *De promissionibus et prædicationibus Dei*. It is the fish of Tobias by which the evil spirit was driven away, and by which sight was restored to Tobit.

So the great Fish cast seven devils out of Mary, gave the tribute-money for Himself and Peter, and restored sight to Paul. He satisfied His disciples with Himself on the shore [of the lake], and shows Himself to all the world as the Fish, by Whose inner remedies we are enlightened and nurtured every day.[2]

Cf. the inscription of Autun, p. 103.

The fish also represents the baptized Christian. In the Catacomb of S. Callixtus there are series of frescoes representing the Sacraments, and in one a fisherman is seen drawing a fish out of the water, and near by a boy being baptized.

We have seen how S. Clement addresses our Lord as the Fisher of Men. S. Hilary applies the figure to the Apostles as it is applied in the Gospels.

The future work of the Apostles is set forth, in drawing men like fish from out of the sea into the light of the heavenly habitation.[3]

Tertullian, however, applies the figure in an opposite sense : " We, little fishes, in accordance with our Fish, JESUS CHRIST, are born in the

[1] *P.L.* xxvi. col. 127. [2] *P.L.* li. col. 816.
[3] *P.L.* ix. col. 931.

water, nor are we safe except by abiding in the water," i.e. except by abiding in that state into which we have been brought by Baptism.[1]

The Dolphin

This is one of the symbols which were taken over by the Christians from pagan art, and adapted to Christian use.

The ancients held the dolphin in high esteem as the friend and preserver of man, who rescues the shipwrecked mariner, and bears him on his back to a place of safety. On the pagan sarcophagi the course of the dolphin over the waves represented the journey of the soul towards the Isles of the Blessed.

Such ideas might naturally suggest to the Christians the appropriateness of the dolphin as a symbol of the Saviour, and the more so since it so closely resembled the symbol of the fish.

In a fresco of the second century a dolphin on a trident appears, signifying Christ Who saves mankind by His Cross. (S. Callixtus.)

The Orante

The figure to which this name is given is one of the very earliest as it is one of the commonest of the figures portrayed in the Catacombs. It is usually that of a woman with a veil falling on either side of the head on to the shoulders, standing with the arms outstretched on either side and the hands uplifted.

Whilst by some she is thought to represent the Church, she is more usually regarded as

[1] *P.L.* i. col. 1198.

TWO FIGURES OF THE ORANTE IN PARADISE.
IN *S. CALLIXTUS*.
3RD CENTURY.

facing p. 50.

CHRISTIAN SYMBOLS

representing the soul of the departed in the attitude of worship. Cf. 1 Tim. ii. 8. Standing was the posture of communicants at the altar, and the posture of prayer on all Sundays and during the festal season from Easter to Pentecost. Irenæus [1] and Tertullian [2] are among the witnesses for this practice; and standing was expressly commanded by the Council of Nicæa (20th Canon), A.D. 325. S. Augustine says:

> We pray standing, which is a sign of the resurrection; whence also the same is observed at the altar on all Lord's days.[3]

The reason here given for its observance would explain why standing in the posture of prayer appeared the most suitable manner of representing the soul which had passed through death to the worship of Heaven among the saints in the Presence of God.

Justin regards hands outstretched in prayer as an imitation of the Cross.[4]

And Tertullian says that we pray not only with uplifted but with open hands, according to the manner of the Passion of the Lord.[5]

---

[1] *P.G.* vi. col. 1364.
[2] *P.L.* i. col. 1191, ii. col. 79.
[3] *P.L.* xxxiii. col. 218.
[4] *Dial.* 90.
[5] *P.L.* i. col. 1169.

CHAPTER VIII

SIGNIFICANCE OF SCENES FROM THE OLD TESTAMENT

The Garden of Paradise. The Four Rivers of Eden. The Creation of Man. The Fall. Noah and the Ark. The sacrifice of Isaac. Moses in the presence of God. Moses striking the Rock. Ascension of Elijah. Jonah. Job. Daniel. The Fiery Furnace. Susanna. Tobias.

THE scenes most frequently represented are : The Creation of Adam and Eve, and their temptation. Noah in the Ark and the Dove returning. The Sacrifice of Isaac. Moses striking the Rock. Jonah cast into the Sea, swallowed by the monster, and brought up again on to dry land. Ananias, Azarias, and Misael in the Fiery Furnace. Daniel among the Lions.

THE GARDEN OF PARADISE

The idea of a sacred garden was not uncommon among the nations of antiquity. To the Roman Christians it would be most familiar in the form in which it appears as the garden of Eden in Gen. ii. The home which God had prepared for mankind, the happy abode of innocence and peace, would naturally seem an appropriate image of the home to which the Christian looked forward in the Presence of God. It appears in a developed form in the mosaics in the churches of Rome, and is represented in the earlier days by trees and the four rivers of Eden.

SCENES FROM OLD TESTAMENT

An Orante standing by a tree or amongst trees expresses the conception that the soul of the departed is in Paradise.

Saturus, the companion of S. Perpetua, had a vision in which he seemed already to have suffered martyrdom and to be borne by angels to a broad place like a garden where were rose-trees and all manner of flowers, and trees tall as cypresses. And he heard voices which sang all together, "Holy, holy, holy," without ceasing.[1]

S. Augustine prays for his friend Verecundus, who had died: "Requite unto Verecundus for his country-house ... where we found rest from the turmoil of the world, the delight of Paradise which blossometh ever."[2]

The Liturgy of the Coptic Jacobites has a prayer for "those who have gone to their rest in the faith of Christ":

Nourish them in a place of pasturage beside the waters of comfort, in the paradise of joy, whence sorrow and sighing have fled away, in the light of Thy saints.[3]

THE FOUR RIVERS OF EDEN

These became a favourite subject in Christian art (see pp. 105 ff.). Thus the Figure of our Lord is seen with the four rivers flowing from beneath His feet; or the rivers are represented as streaming from a hill on which the Lamb of God is standing, or above which there stands the Cross.

They were regarded as types of the living

---

[1] *P.L.* iii. col. 42.
[2] *Confessions*, ix. 3; *P.L.* xxxii. col. 765.
[3] Brightman, *Eastern Liturgies*, p. 170.

water found in the four Gospels, and the water of Baptism brought by them.

S. Cyprian writes:

> The Church setting forth the likeness of Paradise encloses within her walls fruit-bearing trees. . . . These she waters with four rivers, that is, with the four Gospels, wherewith by a celestial inundation she bestows the grace of saving Baptism.[1]

The Gelasian Sacramentary has these words spoken at the blessing of the water of Baptism:

> God in the beginning of His word separated thee from the earth, and dividing thee into four rivers, commanded thee to water the whole earth.[2]

The Creation of Man

Occasionally a group of figures is represented of which one is seated with two small naked figures before him, and of these one is standing, and the other lying on the ground. This is probably intended to signify the creation of Eve.

On a sarcophagus in the Lateran Museum two other large figures appear, of which one is placing his hand on the head of Eve. It has been conjectured that these three large figures may be intended to signify that the Three Persons of the Trinity took part in the creation of mankind.

The Creation of Man is repeatedly brought forward as an argument for the resurrection of the body. So Athenagoras in his treatise on the Resurrection. God, he says, is wise, and no

---

[1] *P.L.* iii. col. 1161, about A.D. 256.
[2] *P.L.* lxxiv. col. 1111.

SARCOPHAGUS IN THE CHRISTIAN MUSEUM OF THE LATERAN

FROM *THE OLD BASILICA OF S. PAOLO*

SUBJECTS REPRESENTED: LEFT TO RIGHT. TOP: CREATION OF EVE. TASKS ASSIGNED TO ADAM AND EVE. TEMPTATION OF EVE. THE MIRACLE OF CANA. THE MIRACLE OF THE LOAVES AND FISHES. THE RAISING OF LAZARUS. BOTTOM: THE MAGI. HEALING OF THE BLIND MAN. DANIEL AND THE LIONS, WITH HABAKKUK. CHRIST WARNING S. PETER. S. PETER TAKEN TO PRISON (?) MOSES STRIKING THE ROCK.

facing p. 54.

SCENES FROM OLD TESTAMENT

work of wisdom is in vain. Therefore He cannot have made man in vain and to no purpose. To man, made in His image, He has assigned a never-ending existence, and has created for him a body corresponding to his soul, a body which undergoes changes such as age or appearance until the last change of all, the resurrection. "We stedfastly hope for a continuance of being in immortality . . . and our belief rests on a most infallible guarantee, the purpose of Him Who fashioned us, according to which He made man of an immortal soul and a body . . . and furnished him with everything belonging to perpetuity," so that the resurrection is seen to be clearly proved by the cause of man's creation and the purpose of Him Who made him.[1]

Again S. Irenæus: If God in the beginning could take dust and form man and cause him to have being who as yet was not, can He not restore what He has made? "What is there then that can keep the flesh from partaking of immortality, which is the blessed and never-ending life given by God?"[2]

Tertullian, arguing against those who held the human body in contempt and as destined to perish utterly, calls to mind the creation of man as showing that the body of man, though made of clay, was fashioned by the hand of God, by His eye, His labour, His purpose, His wisdom, His providence, and above all, His love, and made in His image, which is that which was to become the image of Christ incarnate. The clay was made glorious by the hand of God,

[1] *De Resur.* 12, 13 ; *P.G.* vi. cols. 996–1000.
[2] *Adv. Haer.* v. 3, 2, 3 ; *P.G.* vii. cols. 1130–2.

and the flesh more glorious still by His breathing upon it, by virtue of which it took on itself the ornaments of the soul, of which it is the minister and associate.

And if all this in temporal things, why not also in things eternal ? . . . Shall that very flesh which the Divine Creator formed with His own hands in the image of God, which He animated with His own afflatus, . . . which He set over all the works of His hands, . . . shall it not rise again ? God forbid that He should abandon to everlasting destruction the labour of His own hands, the care of His own thoughts, the receptacle of His own spirit.[1]

THE FALL AND EXPULSION FROM PARADISE

On the sarcophagus mentioned on p. 54 the Creation of Man is followed by a group which is believed to continue the story of Adam and Eve. Between them stands a figure giving to Adam some ears of corn, and to Eve a fleece. This is interpreted as signifying the tasks assigned to them. Next comes the tree round which the serpent is twined in the act of tempting Eve.

The Fall and the Expulsion from Paradise emphasize the penalty of disobedience, but they also recall the truth of the Redemption, and the hope of the Resurrection.

So S. Irenæus: Adam and Eve received as the punishment of their transgression toilsome tasks, and the sentence of returning to dust again. But—

He drove Adam out of Paradise, and removed

[1] *P.L.* ii. col. 802.

SCENES FROM OLD TESTAMENT

him far from the tree of life, not because He envied him, . . . but because He pitied him, . . . and He set a bound to his sin by interposing death, and thus causing sin to cease, putting an end to it by the dissolution of the flesh, . . . so that man, ceasing at length to live to sin, and dying to it, might begin to live to God. . . . Adam had been conquered, all life having been taken from him. When the foe was conquered in his turn, Adam received new life, and the last enemy, Death, is destroyed.[1]

In the *Apostolic Constitutions*, v. 7: He Who formed Man out of earth, and made him a living soul, and Who—

after his disobedience said: "Earth thou art, and to earth thou shalt return," He it is Who also gave us the promise of the Resurrection, for He saith: "All that are in the graves shall hear the voice of the Son of God, and they that hear shall live." And besides this, we believe in the Resurrection because of the Lord's Resurrection. He it is Who raised Lazarus on the fourth day, and the daughter of Jairus, and the widow's son, and raised Himself by the command of the Father after three days, the earnest of our resurrection. For He saith: "I am the Resurrection and the Life." He brought Jonah after three days alive and unscathed out of the belly of the whale, and the three children out of the furnace of Babylonia, and Daniel out of the mouth of the lions, and He will not lack the power to raise us up also."[2]

S. Macrina in her dying prayer:

Thou that didst break the flaming sword, and didst restore to Paradise the man who was crucified

---
[1] *Adv. Haer.* iii. 23, 3–7; *P.G.* vii. col. 962.
[2] *P.G.* i. col. 844.

NOAH

Noah and his ark appear among the most ancient of the frescoes, i.e. those of the first century (S. Domitilla). The subject was clearly a favourite one, for it is found again and again in the Catacombs. Noah is often depicted as rising out of what looks like a box.

The application to the condition of the Church in the early centuries is obvious. In the Church, as in the ark, men found a refuge in the midst of an evil and a troubled world. There they dwelt in safety under God's protection.

The Ark, then, signifies the Church, according to Tertullian.[2]

And S. Cyprian writes:

> He cannot have God for his Father who has not the Church for his mother. If any who were outside the ark of Noah could escape, then he may escape who is outside the Church.[3]

In 1 Peter iii. 20, the salvation of those who took refuge in the ark from the waters of the flood is likened to the salvation of those who in their Baptism make the response of a good conscience to the question addressed to them.[4] Such at least is a probable meaning of this difficult verse.

To the writer of the Epistle to the Hebrews [5] Noah is the pattern of those who listen to the Divine voice and make preparation for "things not yet seen." So the thought expressed in the

---

[1] *P.G.* xlvi col. 984.　　[2] *P.L.* i. col. 1209.
[3] *P.L.* iv. col. 519.　　[4] See p. 95.　　[5] xi. 7.

SCENES FROM OLD TESTAMENT

frescoes may well have looked to the unseen world and the abode of peace and safety into which the faithful departed have entered.

For other ideas which came to be connected with this story, see under DOVE, p. 87.

THE SACRIFICE OF ISAAC

This subject is represented in one of the Chapels of the Sacraments in S. Callixtus (about A.D. 200) and very frequently elsewhere.

It was commonly regarded as a type of the Passion of our Lord. E.g. Tertullian writes that Isaac was led as a sacrifice by his father, and bore the wood for the offering of himself, thus pointing to the death of Christ, delivered up by His Father as a victim, and bearing the heavy load of the wood of His Passion.[1]

In one painting Abraham and Isaac appear as if in the act of giving thanks. (S. Callixtus.) Here then the peril is passed, and the scene would thus be one of those which were recalled as showing how God saves His people from the very jaws of death.

That this subject may have had a further significance is suggested by Heb. xi. 19. Parents who were obliged to give up their children to suffer death for Christ's sake might find in this verse an encouragement to believe that they would receive them back, " accounting that God is able to raise up even from the dead."

S. Ambrose speaks of the story of Gen. xxii. as foreshadowing that other Sacrifice Whom God would provide for all mankind, for Whom

[1] *P.L.* ii. col. 626.

fathers would offer their sons, and not fear to part from them in this world. How many fathers, when their sons have suffered martyrdom, have returned from their graves with gladness ! [1]

Moses Loosening his Sandals

In a few frescoes a man is represented with his foot raised, and apparently in the act of removing his sandals. In one a hand is stretched out towards him from the sky. (S. Callixtus.) This is thought to be intended for Moses (of whom another picture appears in the same place) either before the Burning Bush or preparing to ascend Mount Sinai to receive the Law. In either case the thought would be the reverence and awe with which he stood in the presence of God, and so would be an appropriate type of the soul coming to appear before God.

So in the prayer for the departed in the Gelasian Sacramentary :

Receive, O Lord, the soul of thy servant . . . and give it a place among those who see God face to face.[2]

Moses Striking the Rock

This scene forms one of the favourite subjects of early Christian art, being represented no less than sixty-eight times in the Catacombs.

Its significance was already present to the mind of S. Paul when he wrote 1 Cor. x. :

They did all eat the same spiritual meat; and did all drink the same spiritual drink: for they drank of a spiritual rock that followed them : and the rock was Christ.

---

[1] *P.L.* xiv. col. 447. [2] *P.L.* lxxiv. col. 1233.

SCENES FROM OLD TESTAMENT

This he applies to the Christian Sacraments.

S. Augustine, quoting these words, says that as the rock was struck with a rod of wood that the water might flow out, so the Cross came to Christ that He might give us to drink of His grace.[1]

Wilpert explains this subject as having a threefold significance. After the middle of the third century it was applied, as by S. Augustine, to the refreshment of the soul by the water of life given by Christ. Again, as the children of Israel were saved from dying of thirst by the water flowing from the rock, so it typified the deliverance of the soul from eternal death. But he is of opinion that the water flowing from the rock was at first always connected with Baptism.

If it seem strange that this figure of drinking should have been thought an appropriate image of Baptism, yet it is clear that it was so regarded in the early Church, that is, Baptism as the water of life which quenches the thirst of the soul.

In the ancient baptistery of S. Priscilla the words were written: " Let him that is athirst come."

Tertullian writes thus:

This is the water which flowed down to the people from the rock that went with them. For if the rock is Christ, we see without a doubt that Baptism is blessed by the water in Christ.[2]

S. Cyprian writes that God had declared

[1] *P.L.* xxxviii. col. 1553.   [2] *P.L.* i. col. 1210.

EARLY CHRISTIANS OF ROME

beforehand by the prophet that copious streams should flow in the desert to give drink to the elect family of God, i.e. those who by being born in Baptism become the sons of God. And referring to Isa. xlviii. 21, he says that this was fulfilled in the Gospel when Christ, Who is the Rock, was pierced with a lance. And this the Lord had foretold when He said, "If any man thirst, let him come unto Me, and drink," for He was speaking of Baptism, in which the Holy Spirit is received.[1]

Hence in the Gelasian Sacramentary, at the blessing of the Baptismal water the words were said:

I bless thee ... through the living God ... Who ... in the desert brought water out of the rock for the people who were athirst.[2]

Wilpert points out that the figure of Moses resembles the traditional figure of S. Peter, and refers to some glasses in the Vatican Museum on which this scene is depicted, and above the figure striking the rock the name Petrus is written.[3] He quotes Maximus of Turin (fifth century) as saying that—

the rock (*petra*) was Christ as Paul taught, so Petrus was made *petra* by Christ, Who said, "On this rock (*petra*) I will build My Church"; for as in the desert water flowed from the rock for the people who were athirst, so from the mouth of Peter flowed the fountain of the health-giving confession to the whole world.[4]

[1] *P.L.* iv. col. 379.
[2] *P.L.* lxxiv. col. 1110.
[3] *Principienfragen.*, p. 29.
[4] *P.L.* lvii. col. 394.

SCENES FROM OLD TESTAMENT

The Ascension of Elijah

This scene appears twice in the Catacombs and several times on the sarcophagi. On one of these Elijah is shown going up to heaven in the chariot, and leaving his mantle to Elisha. (Lateran Museum.)

Enoch and Elijah were naturally regarded as outstanding examples of the power of God to preserve His servants in body as well as in soul, and hence as evidence for the resurrection of the body.

So S. Irenæus:

Enoch was translated in the same body in which he had pleased God, thus pointing out by anticipation the translation of the just. And Elijah was caught up in his bodily form, thus exhibiting in prophecy the assumption of those who are spiritual, and that nothing stood in the way of their body being translated and caught up.[1]

Tertullian refers to Enoch and Elijah as learning to the full what it is for the flesh to be exempted from all humiliation, and loss, and injury, and disgrace, translated as they have been from this world, without passing through death and resurrection, thus testifying to the completeness of our life hereafter.[2]

Jonah

That the story of Jonah's marvellous deliverance from death had vividly impressed the minds of the early Christians is evident from the frequent references to it in their writings, and the frequency with which it appears in the Cata-

[1] *P.G.* vii. col. 1134.   [2] *P.L.* ii. col. 881.

combs and on the sarcophagi. Here Jonah is
seen being cast into the sea, swallowed by the
monster, cast up on the land, and reposing under
the gourd. To the Christians this appeared a
most convincing proof of the resurrection, since
it proved God's power to bring His servants
through death into life.

So Tertullian in his treatise on the Resurrection of the Flesh, ch. 58. And again in ch. 32,
where he argues from the case of Jonah that
there will be a resurrection even of those whose
bodies have been devoured by beasts or fishes.[1]

And S. Irenæus :

Jonah when he had been cast into the deep and
swallowed down into the whale's belly, was thrown
up safe on to the land by the command of God.
And again Ananias, Azarias, and Misael were cast
into the furnace heated sevenfold, and remained
unscathed, neither was the smell of fire upon them,
. . . and all of these came forth unhurt, led as it
were by the hand of God to show forth His power ;
so now although some . . . deem it impossible for
God, Who raises the dead, to have power to confer
upon them eternal duration, yet their unbelief
shall not make the faithfulness of God of none
effect.[2]

And Pseudo-Cyprian :

As Thou hearkenedst to Jonah out of the belly
of the whale, even so hearken unto me, and bring
me forth out of death into life.[3]

See also the reference in the *Apostolic Constitutions* given above, p. 57.

[1] *P.L.* ii. col. 840.   [2] *P.G.* vii. col. 1135.
[3] *P.L.* iv. col. 987.

SCENES FROM OLD TESTAMENT

JOB

Occasionally a figure is represented sitting alone on a heap or a stool. In one fresco, however, a woman is shown holding out to him what appears to be a loaf on the end of a rod (SS. Pietro e Marcellino). On the sarcophagus of Junius Bassus she is represented as covering her mouth with her mantle. This suggests that the solitary sufferer is Job afflicted with an obnoxious disease. If so, the reason for his appearance on tombs may be to show the sufferings of the righteous and their final deliverance, even as Job was at last delivered out of all his calamities.

A further reason may have been that Job was regarded as the witness of the resurrection, as by S. Clement of Rome: " Again Job saith : And Thou shalt raise this my flesh which hath endured all these things." [1]

DANIEL IN THE LIONS' DEN, AND THE THREE YOUNG MEN IN THE FIERY FURNACE

Both these subjects are among the earliest frescoes in the Catacombs, and are very frequently represented in frescoes and on the sarcophagi. The figure of Daniel with the lions made of gilded bronze is said by Eusebius to have been set up by the Emperor Constantine on the fountains of Constantinople.[2]

Many references to both stories are found in early Christian writings, and they are often mentioned together, as by S. Clement of Rome in his Epistle to the Corinthians, 45. See also

[1] Job xix. 26 in the Greek. Lightfoot, p. 19.
[2] *Vita Constant.* iii. 49; *P.G.* xx. col. 1110.

the reference in the *Apostolic Constitutions* above, p. 57.

The reason for the prominence given to them has been already suggested (p. 38). So Origen writes :

> Not alone did Nebuchadnezzar of old set up the golden image. Not then alone did he threaten Azarias, Ananias, and Misael that if they would not worship it they should be cast into the fiery furnace. But even now Nebuchadnezzar says the same things to us.

With Daniel, he proceeds, let us slay the dragon, so that when we draw near to the mouth of the lions we may suffer no hurt.[1]

The father of Origen had died a martyr's death.

S. Cyprian addressed a letter to Lucius, Bishop of Rome, on his return from exile. Though he and his companions, says S. Cyprian, had been prepared to suffer to the uttermost, God had brought him back to his people with no less honour than if he had been a martyr as well as a confessor.

> For the dignity of martyrdom was not the less in the case of the three children, because their death being frustrated, they came forth safe from the fiery furnace. Nor did Daniel stand forth incomplete in the praise he deserved, because when he had been sent to the lions for a prey he was protected by the Lord and lived to glory. Among the confessors of Christ martyrdoms deferred do not lessen the merit of confession, but show forth the greatness of Divine protection. We see repre-

[1] *P.G.* xi. 604. The reference to Daniel is to be found in *Bel and the Dragon*, 23 ff.

SCENES FROM OLD TESTAMENT

sented in you what the brave and illustrious youths announced before the king, that they indeed were prepared to be burned in the flames that they might not serve his gods, nor worship the image which he had made, but that the God Whom they worshipped and Whom we also worship, was able even to rescue them from the fiery furnace, and to deliver them from the hands of the king.[1]

The work *De laude martyrii* is included among the pseudo-Cyprianic writings. Harnack conjectures [2] that the author was the Roman presbyter Novatian, about A.D. 250. He writes:

Daniel, by the constancy of his faith, overcame the threats of the king and the fury of raging lions, in that he believed that none else than God was to be adored. Thus when the young men were thrown into the furnace ... they endured the flames, ... believing in God.... God saw their faith, that what they had promised to themselves to see after their death, they merited to see in their body.... For there was one mind to all of them, which neither violence could break down nor wrath subvert; nor could the fear of death restrain them from the obedience of devotion.[3]

It is clear that these stories must often have inspired the martyrs with courage and strength in the face of death.

The figure that occasionally appears with Daniel on the sarcophagi is supposed to be the prophet Habakkuk. See *Bel and the Dragon*, 33. There is a reference to this in the prayer included in the pseudo-Cyprianic writings:

[1] *P.L.* iii. col. 1003.
[2] *Chronologie der altchristlichen Litteratur*, ii. 404.
[3] *P.L* .iv. col. 824.

EARLY CHRISTIANS OF ROME

Hearken to me as I pray, even as Thou heardest the three children out of the furnace of fire ... and didst send Thine angel with a cloud of moisture.... Hearken to me as I pray, as Thou didst hearken to Daniel, out of the lions' den, and didst send Habakkuk the prophet, and he brought him food, and said, " Eat the food which God hath sent thee." And Daniel said, " God will not forsake those who seek Him." [1]

The angel is also sometimes represented.

SUSANNA AND THE ELDERS

This subject is represented five times in the Catacombs.

In one fresco (S. Prætextatus) instead of the figure of Susanna and the two men, a lamb is shown standing between two wolves, and the names are written above: *Susanna, Senioris.* She is the type of the innocent assailed by the wicked who plot against them, and seek to corrupt them, but whose evil designs are frustrated, for the Lord hears the cry of His people and rescues them from their enemies.

Hearken unto my prayer even as Thou didst hearken unto Susanna, when she was in the power of the elders; even so deliver me from this [evil] world, for thou lovest a pure conscience.—*Pseudo-Cyprian.*[2]

Hippolytus interprets the story as follows: Susanna is a figure of the Church; the two elders are figures of the two peoples that plot against the Church, i.e. the Jews and the Gentiles. When they conspire together to

[1] *P.L.* iv. col. 987.   [2] *P.L.* iv. 988.

SCENES FROM OLD TESTAMENT

destroy any of the saints, they lie in wait till they can seize them and carry them off, saying, "Come and worship our gods; and if not, we will bear witness against you." And when they refuse, they drag them before the court, and accuse them of acting contrary to the decrees of Cæsar, and condemn them to death. But Susanna deemed it better to die by the hand of wicked men and live with God, than by consenting unto them to be delivered from them but to fall into the hands of God. And the Christian who forsakes his faith is given over to death, but those who call upon God from a pure heart He heareth.[1]

TOBIAS AND THE FISH

This subject is represented in three paintings in the Catacombs. In one of these Tobias is holding up the fish before the angel, who stands with his hand stretched out towards it. (Cemetery of Thrason.) The story was interpreted, as we have seen (p. 49), as signifying the power of Christ to drive away evil spirits, and restore sight to the blind. But the original intention may have been to depict that part of the story in which the fish appears as the enemy from which Tobias was delivered by the help of the angel, thus signifying the perils through which the Christian passes on his journey through life, and the heavenly power which guides and guards him.

"As Thou wast with Tobias, even so vouchsafe to be with me," is the petition in the pseudo-Cyprianic prayer.[2]

[1] *P.G.* x. col. 689.   [2] *P.L.* iv. col. 986.

CHAPTER IX

SIGNIFICANCE OF SCENES FROM THE NEW TESTAMENT

The Mother of our Lord. The Magi. The Feast at Cana. The woman of Samaria. The paralytic. The feeding of the multitudes. The blind receiving sight. The raising of Lazarus. The denial of S. Peter. Pilate.

THE MOTHER OF OUR LORD

ACCORDING to Wilpert,[1] the Mother of our Lord is not represented in the Catacombs without Him, except at the Annunciation. The earliest picture is believed to be that in the Catacomb of S. Priscilla, of the first half of the second century. She appears with the Holy Child in her arms, and beside them is a standing figure pointing to a star which has now almost faded away. Wilpert is of opinion that the standing figure is intended for a prophet, as it is shown wearing a long mantle and holding a roll; and this prophet is probably Isaiah, who was believed to have foretold the birth of Christ, and to have also foretold that He would be the Light of the world.

It might be thought that the figure is meant to recall the utterance of Balaam: "A star shall arise out of Jacob"; but Justin quotes Isaiah as saying:

A star shall rise out of Jacob, and a flower shall spring from the root of Jesse. . . . And a star of light

[1] *Malereien*, vol. i, p. 186.

has arisen, and a flower has sprung from the root of Jesse, this Christ.

And he proceeds to quote Isaiah's words: "Behold, a virgin shall conceive, and bear a son."[1]

The inscriptions which have been given above (p. 29) will have shown the belief that our Lord is not only the Light of this world, but the Light of the faithful in the life beyond death.

The Magi

This subject appears in the Catacomb of S. Priscilla as early as the beginning of the second century. Perhaps no scene has been more frequently represented in Christian art. In these early pictures the Blessed Virgin is seated with the Holy Child, whilst the Magi approach bearing their gifts. Occasionally the star is found. In this way the painters and sculptors expressed the belief that He Who was born of the Virgin was entitled, even whilst yet an infant, to receive the homage of mankind, and had come to be " a light to lighten the Gentiles." This belief could be appropriately expressed by the Oriental dress of the Magi, their gifts, and the star. The story would make a special appeal to Christians of non-Jewish race.

Justin connects the prophecy of the birth of Emmanuel with Isa. viii. 4, which he renders: "He shall take the power of Damascus and spoils of Samaria in presence of the king of Assyria." And he argues that as this had not been fulfilled in the case of any child among the

[1] *Apol.* i. 32.

Jews, the prophet must have been speaking of the birth of Christ and the coming of the Magi from Arabia to worship Him, for Damascus, he says, is in the region of Arabia.[1]

Irenæus refers to the Magi as led by a star to Emmanuel, the Son of the Virgin, Who was also the Son of God—

And they showed by their gifts Who it was that was worshipped: myrrh because it was He Who should die for the human race, gold because He was the King of Whose kingdom there should be no end, and frankincense because He was God, made known in Judæa, and declared to those who sought Him not."[2]

The *Missale Gothicum* has this Collect for Epiphany:

Almighty and eternal God, Who madest Thy power known among the nations, and hast manifested Thy salvation to all peoples, setting forth this day when a star surpassing all other stars in brightness led men summoned from other regions of the earth to adore the childhood of Him Who is the true King, and when the beam of Thy light made manifest Him Who is the Lord of heaven and earth, born for the salvation of all men. Wherefore all the world exulteth in the joys Thou hast shed abroad; yea, and the heavenly powers sing the praise of Thy glory, saying without ceasing, Holy, holy, holy.[3]

THE MARRIAGE FEAST AT CANA

The beginning of the signs in which "Jesus manifested His glory" to the first disciples was

---

[1] *Dial.* 77, 78.
[2] *Adv. Haer.* iii. 9, 2; *P.G.* vii. col. 870.
[3] *P.L.* lxxii. col. 241.

taken by those who came after as a signal proof of His power.

So the Gelasian Sacramentary at the hallowing of the water for Baptism:

I bless thee through Jesus Christ, Who in Cana of Galilee by a marvellous sign through His power changed thee into wine.[1]

In the *Apostolic Constitutions* (v. 7) it is applied to the resurrection: "He Who changed water into wine, He will also raise the dead to life."[2]

Again, the miracle is interpreted as showing the power of Christ to make the Eucharistic wine His Blood.

In the cemetery of SS. Pietro e Marcellino the feast of Cana is represented with the guests seated at a table, whilst in the foreground a figure larger than the rest, the figure of Christ, appears holding in His hand a rod with which He is touching the six water-pots. Above is an Orante, which may be meant to signify the communion of the soul with God.

As Moses of old had wrought wonders by means of his rod, so Christ is often shown holding a rod when He is doing His three wonderful works, viz. changing the water into wine, multiplying the loaves and fishes, and raising Lazarus. But in wonders wrought upon living people He is shown as placing His hand upon them, even when with the other hand He holds the rod.

S. Cyril of Jerusalem, speaking of the assurance with which communicants should receive

[1] *P.L.* lxxiv. col. 1111.   [2] *P.G.* i. col. 852.

the Body and Blood of Christ in the Eucharist, says:

> He Who once by His own will changed the water into wine at Cana of Galilee, is He not worthy of our faith when changing wine into His Blood?[1]

Epiphany was regarded as the commemoration of this miracle, and in the *Missale Gothicum* a prayer for use at Epiphany asks that He Who then changed water into wine may now convert the wine of the oblations into His Blood.[2]

See further under EUCHARIST, p. 102.

CHRIST AT THE WELL OF SAMARIA

This scene which appears in the Catacombs (S. Callixtus) and on the sarcophagi receives its explanation from our Lord's words to the woman of Samaria (S. John iv.). He is the Giver of the water of life which satisfies the thirst of the soul. S. John vii. 38 should also be understood as signifying that He is the fountain from which flow the rivers of living water. Cf. the reference on p. 103 to "the immortal gift to mortals, the God-given waters, the ever-flowing waters of wealth-giving wisdom." Here the reference is clearly the same.

This, then, is the image used to describe the blessedness of the faithful departed. It corresponds to the prayers that the spirit may be refreshed which we have seen in the inscriptions. So S. Perpetua in her vision saw her young brother who had died, drinking from a fountain, and he was refreshed.[3]

[1] *P.G.* xxxiii. col. 1098. [2] *P.L.* lxxii. col. 242.
[3] *P.L.* iii. col. 39.

SCENES FROM NEW TESTAMENT

In some cases it applies specially to martyrs, both before and after their martyrdom. The Epistle of the Gallican Churches (A.D. 177) describes the tortures inflicted on the martyr Sanctus, but—

he remained unmoved and unyielding, stedfast in his confession, refreshed and strengthened by the heavenly fountain of the water of life which proceeds from the heart of Christ.[1]

Marianus, who suffered martyrdom in A.D. 259, had a vision in which he appeared to be walking with S. Cyprian (martyred the year before) through pleasant meadows and verdant groves, till they came to a fountain brimming with pure water. S. Cyprian filled a bowl with the water and drank, and filled it again and gave it to him, and he drank it eagerly, saying: "Thanks be to God."[2]

S. John likewise describes the blessedness of those who have "come out of great tribulation":

They shall hunger no more, neither thirst any more ... For the Lamb ... shall guide them unto fountains of waters of life (Rev. vii. 17).

S. Cyprian interprets our Lord's words in S. John iv. as referring to Baptism:

For the Lord said, ... Whosoever drinketh of the water that I shall give him, shall never thirst. By which is signified the very Baptism of saving

[1] Euseb. *H.E.* v. i.
[2] *Passio SS. Mariani et Jacobi.* Pio Franchi de' Cavalieri, p. 54.

water, which is received once for all and never repeated.[1]

The Paralytic

The man who carried his bed is often seen on the monuments. Such an incident is twice mentioned in the Gospels: S. Mark ii. 12 and S. John v. 9. The reference in the *Apostolic Constitutions*, v. 7, might equally well have either passage in view: "He Who set the paralytic in soundness upon his feet . . . He Himself will call us back to Life."[2] Here, then, the miracle is applied to the Resurrection.

Elsewhere, however, stress is laid on the mention, in certain MSS. of the Gospel, of the angel who by troubling the water effected the healing of the sick. During the first two centuries this was interpreted as a type of Baptism, as by Tertullian, who says that the angel stirred the pool, and the sick in body were healed. In Baptism the spirit is healed and for ever, and such cures are effected every day, death being blotted out by the washing away of offences.[3]

So also S. Ambrose:

For them an angel came down; for you [i.e. in Baptism] the Holy Ghost. . . . Then only one was healed, now all Christian people are made whole. . . . For that pool was a figure that you may believe that the Divine power comes down upon this font. The paralytic waited for a man. And who was that man but the Lord, . . . at Whose coming the truth should heal all men?[4]

[1] *P.L.* iv. 391.
[2] *P.G.* i. col. 851.
[3] *P.L.* i. col. 1206.
[4] *P.L.* xvi. col. 395.

SCENES FROM NEW TESTAMENT

The prayer at the blessing of the font in the *Missale Gothicum*:

Thou that providest the waters of Bethsaida through the healing operation of the angel, . . . grant that the angel of Thy fatherly love may be present to this holy fount. . . . Bless . . . this water which Thou hast created; let Thy power descend upon it. Pour into it from above the Holy Spirit, the angel of truth.[1]

Wilpert, however, considers that after the third century the painters of the Catacombs mostly intend to represent the paralytic of S. Mark ii. and thereby to express faith in the Divinity of Christ.[2]

THE FEEDING OF THE MULTITUDES

The monuments have a considerable number of representations of this subject. Christ is seen holding in His hand the rod with which He is touching the baskets of loaves placed before Him. Occasionally He is seen touching them with His hand. On a sarcophagus in the Lateran Museum He stands between two disciples with one hand on the loaves and the other on the fishes. Baskets of bread, usually seven or twelve (in accordance with S. Mark viii. 8 and vi. 43), are also represented.

This is one of the signs to which reference is made in the *Apostolic Constitutions* as showing that the power of Christ is sufficient to raise the dead.[3]

But the dominant idea with which this sign

[1] *P.L.* lxxii. col. 274.   [2] *Malereien*, p. 218.
[3] v. 7; *P.G.* i. col. 852.

was associated is that given in the interpretation by the fourth Evangelist. (S. John vi.) It signifies Christ Who gives to hungering multitudes throughout the world the unfailing supply of heavenly Food, which is Himself, the Bread of Life and the Cup of Life.

So S. Ambrose:

He it is Who fed four thousand people in the desert with five loaves and two fishes, and could have fed more had there been more who needed to be fed. And now not bread made out of barley is given as food, but His own Body out of heaven.[1]

As this miracle became the habitual type of the Eucharist, see further, pp. 100, 102.

Christ Giving Sight to the Blind

In this scene, which appears in several frescoes and sarcophagi, Christ is represented as laying His hand on the eyes of the blind man. Irenæus unfolds the significance of this action in the case of the man who had been born blind (S. John ix.) by saying that Christ gave him sight, not by His word, as in some cases of healing, but by anointing his eyes with clay that He might thus show forth the hand of God which at the beginning had moulded man out of clay.

And inasmuch as man ... having fallen into transgression, needed the laver of regeneration, the Lord said to him after He had smeared his eyes with the clay, "Go to Siloam, and wash," thus restoring to him both his complete conformation, and that regeneration which takes place by means of the laver.[2]

[1] *P.L.* xvi. col. 220. [2] *P.G.* vii. col. 1165.

SCENES FROM NEW TESTAMENT

" Illumination " is the term commonly employed in the early Church for Baptism, and those who have been baptized are called " those who have been enlightened." See Heb. vi. 4, " enlightened once for all."

Justin, describing the rite of Baptism, says:

This washing is called illumination, because they who learn these things are illuminated in their understandings.[1]

S. Clement of Alexandria writes:

Being baptized we are illuminated, illuminated we become sons, being made sons we are made perfect, being made perfect we are made immortal. ... This work is variously called grace, and illumination, and perfection, and washing, ... illumination by which that holy light of salvation is beheld, that is, by which we see God clearly. ... We who are baptized ... have the eye of the spirit free, unimpeded, and full of light, by which alone we contemplate the divine, the Holy Spirit flowing down to us from above. ... But the end is reserved till the resurrection of those who believe. ... We, repenting of our sins, renouncing our iniquities, purified by Baptism, speed back to the eternal light, children to the Father.[2]

In the *Apostolic Constitutions*, v. 7, the miracle is also used to teach the doctrine of the resurrection of the body.

He Who gave to the man the organ which had been lacking from his birth, ... He it is Who will call us also back to life.[3]

[1] *Apol.* i. 61.   [2] *P.G.* viii. cols. 281–8.
[3] *P.G.* i. 852.

If even amid the shadows of this life there is given to the faithful, as S. Clement teaches, an illumination by which they see God clearly, what must it be when they have " sped back to the eternal light " ? We have seen the prayer inscribed on a tomb : " May God give thee light." On another is the fine inscription : " Deum videre cupiens vidit " (" Desiring to behold God, he beheld Him "). (S. Domitilla.) And see p. 104 : " Thou Light of the dead."

In the Gelasian Sacramentary we find the prayer for the departed :

O God, the Light of faithful souls, give ear to our supplications, and grant to all those whose bodies rest here, an abode of refreshment, a blessed tranquillity, and the splendour of light.[1]

The Raising of Lazarus

The appropriateness of this subject is so evident that its very frequent appearance in the Catacombs and on the sarcophagi needs no explanation. That this miracle should be preferred to other miracles of the raising of the dead can be accounted for by its more marvellous character, and by the words uttered by our Lord on that occasion : " I am the Resurrection and the Life."

The later representations follow a conventional type. Our Lord stands with His rod outstretched to the tomb, which appears as a small building in the doorway of which Lazarus stands swathed in the grave-clothes.

[1] *P.L.* lxxiv. col. 1241.

SCENES FROM NEW TESTAMENT

The significance of the rod has been already noticed. p. 73.

The Denial of S. Peter

In a fourth-century fresco in the cemetery of S. Cyriaca our Lord is seen addressing S. Peter with His hand raised, as if warning him of the coming temptation. The cock between them shows unmistakably what is the subject represented. It occurs frequently on the sarcophagi. It may at first cause surprise that this scene from the life of S. Peter should be commemorated rather than those which appear to do him greater honour. But if it calls to mind the fall of the Apostle, it also recalls our Lord's intercession on his behalf, and his restoration. It was a true instinct of the early Church which saw in the cock not primarily a reminder of the fall, but of the faith which gave him the strength to rise from his fall and to strengthen his brethren.

Hymn of S. Ambrose for the hour of cock-crow:

> Præco diei jam sonat,
> Noctis profundæ pervigil,
> ....
> Hoc ipse Petra Ecclesiæ
> Canente culpam diluit.
> ....
>
> Gallo canente spes redit,
> Ægris salus refunditur,
> Mucro latronis conditur,
> Lapsis fides revertitur.
>
> Jesu, labantes respice,
> Et nos videndo corrige :
> Si respicis, lapsus cadunt,
> Fletuque culpa solvitur.

EARLY CHRISTIANS OF ROME

Thus Pseudo-Cyprian writes:

The failures of good men, however great, are turned by the Divine Providence to the advancement of the Church. Thus the Prince of the Apostles failed, and Paul, the teacher of the Gentiles, and Mary Magdalene, in whom the Church now glories exceedingly, and their failures have issued in the stablishing and comforting of the House of God.[1]

Those who designed these pictures may have had in mind that the temptation to be unfaithful to their Lord was still a peril to the Christians of their own day. It was well that they should be reminded that even for those who yield to the temptations which beset them in this earthly life, there is a Divine Intercessor, there is forgiveness with God, and restoration.

Accordingly we find in the Liturgies such prayers for the departed as the following, in the Leonian Sacramentary:

O God, to Whom alone it belongeth to impart healing after death, grant, we beseech Thee, that the soul of Thy servant being released from the pollutions of earth may be made a partaker of Thy redemption.[2]

In the Gelasian Sacramentary:

O Lord, we pray Thee, graciously to receive this Oblation which we offer to Thee for those departed, and in Thine abundant compassion grant that by these offerings they may be cleansed from all the stains of their earthly life.[3]

[1] *P.L.* iv. col. 974. [2] *P.L.* lv. col. 135.
[3] *P.L.* lxxiv. col. 1241.

SCENES FROM NEW TESTAMENT

And this from the Liturgy of the Coptic Jacobites :

There is no death unto Thy servants, but a passage : but if some listlessness have seized them or some heedlessness, as men who have worn flesh and dwelt in this world, yet do Thou, as a good God and a Lover of man, vouchsafe to forgive them : for there is none clean from blemish, not even if his life on earth be but one day. To those, O Lord, whose souls Thou hast taken, grant rest ; may they be counted worthy of the kingdom of Heaven.[1]

PILATE WASHING HIS HANDS

The water being brought to Pilate is a scene which is represented several times on the sarcophagi. This incident of the Passion was so distinctive that the figure could be clearly recognized as that of Pilate.

On a sarcophagus in the Lateran Museum Pilate's face is turned away from those standing before him, and wears an expression of doubt and perplexity which is very strikingly portrayed.

The trial before the Roman Governor would naturally be of special interest to the Roman Church. The old Creed of Rome which can be traced back to the second century, the Creed which every Roman Christian learned before his Baptism, contained the words : *Crucified under Pontius Pilate.*

Not only are pictures of the Crucifixion unknown in the Catacombs, but even the cross is disguised, as in the monogram of Christ (p. 43), and in the anchor with its cross-bar, and the

[1] Brightman, *Eastern Liturgies*, p. 170.

EARLY CHRISTIANS OF ROME

trident, or the Greek letter T as it appears inserted in $ITX\Theta\Upsilon\Sigma$.

The reverence with which the early Church regarded the Passion of our Lord, and the horror which death by crucifixion aroused, made it impossible to depict the suffering and the ignominy of the death upon the cross.

A few examples have been found of small gems on which a crucifix is graven. Otherwise it does not appear till the fifth century, and then but rarely. The carving on the doors of S. Sabina on the Aventine may be of the fifth or perhaps of the sixth century. And it was not till the end of the seventh century that pictures of the Crucifixion were definitely authorized.

Even in the eighth century these representations were very far from the stark realism with which we have become familiar in the modern crucifix. At first the Saviour is depicted as alive with the eyes open, and His form as if He were standing before the cross with outstretched arms rather than as hanging upon it. The feet are fastened separately with two nails. In the eighth-century fresco of S. Maria Antiqua He appears wearing a long robe as in other early crucifixes, and the signs expressive of agony and humiliation are conspicuously absent. On one side the soldier is seen holding up the sponge on a rod; on the other, the soldier with the lance piercing our Lord's side. But the picture seems designed to show a Power that no suffering could overcome, and to impress upon the beholder the majesty and eternal glory of the Cross.

CHAPTER X

VARIOUS SYMBOLS

The Anchor. The Dove. The Hart. The Lamb. The Peacock. The Phœnix. The Ship.

WE have now to consider the significance of the representations of certain animals or objects which were used as symbols. That some were recognized as legitimate for Christian uses whereas others were unlawful appears in a passage of the *Pædagogus* of S. Clement of Alexandria, iii. 11. He enumerates the figures which a Christian may have on his seal—a dove, or a fish, or a ship scudding before the wind, or a lyre, or a ship's anchor.[1]

THE ANCHOR

This symbol appears very early and very frequently. It expresses the sure hope of the Christian in the life of the unseen world, as is shown in that Epistle to which reference has already been made as having points of contact with the beliefs expressed on the Roman monuments: Heb. vi. 19.

It has been suggested that the choice of this symbol may be due to the first Christians who came from the East to Rome after a long voyage. The anchor is let down when the ship is near the haven, and is therefore a fitting

[1] *P.G.* viii. col. 633.

symbol of the assurance that the souls of the faithful will come to their desired haven when their journey across the stormy ocean of this life is ended.

It is sometimes found in combination with the word HOPE, or HOPE IN GOD, or HOPE IN CHRIST; and it is often found in combination with the fish, expressing in another way that Christ is the Hope of the Christian.

The anchor with the cross-bar forming a cross has a twofold meaning, viz. that for the Christian the hope in the life beyond is found in the Cross of Christ.

When found with the palm, the anchor expresses the hope of the victory and gladness which await the departed.

The Dove

The dove is not peculiar to Christian monuments; it was used for decorative purposes in pagan art.

After the middle of the second century it appears as a definite Christian symbol, and as such was extensively employed, and not always with the same significance.

1. Where the dove was represented in the scene of our Lord's Baptism, there can, of course, be no doubt of its meaning. Where it appears on some other monuments, the significance may possibly be that expressed in the prayer we have noticed: " Mayest thou live in the Holy Spirit."

2. It may sometimes represent a pure and innocent spirit. This is shown by inscriptions such as " Palumbus sine fel," i.e. " A dove

VARIOUS SYMBOLS

without gall." It was for this reason, says Tertullian, that the Holy Spirit descended upon the Lord in the shape of a dove, that through its simplicity and innocence the nature of the Holy Spirit might be declared.[1]

3. It appears to signify the soul released from the bonds of earthly existence, and free to wing its flight to heavenly regions.

A tablet in the Lateran Museum bearing the name *Magna* shows the Orante standing by a tree on which a dove is sitting.

Another has the figure of the Orante, and beside it a dove sitting on the cage from which it has escaped to take its flight. (Lateran Museum.)

In one picture a dove is shown flying towards the monogram of Christ. "To go away from the body: to come home to the Lord."[2]

4. The dove or two doves are often represented as drinking from a vessel, or as eating grapes or other fruit. Here the idea seems to be that expressed in such petitions as: "May God refresh thy spirit."

5. The dove holding an olive branch, the dove being received by Noah into the ark—these represent the soul which has passed over the waves of the flood, and has reached at last a place of peace and safety. We are reminded of the words IN PACE, inscribed on countless Christian tombs, and on one monument in the Lateran Museum by the side of the dove and the olive branch the word PAX is written.

In a fresco in the cemetery of S. Priscilla the fiery furnace and the three children are depicted,

[1] *P.L.* i. col. 1208.   [2] 2 Cor. v. 8.

and above them the dove with the olive branch. Is this to signify the peace that comes to those who are faithful unto death?

One tablet has the fish and two doves, symbolizing that the souls of the faithful rest in the peace of Christ.

In S. Callixtus a ship is represented coming into port, and on the prow a dove with an olive branch, signifying the end of the journey of the faithful soul when it arrives in peace in the celestial haven.

6. Tertullian sees in the return of the dove a type of the peace which comes to the soul in Baptism. As after the waters of the Flood, a Baptism, as it were, of the world, for the putting away of sin, a dove was sent forth to proclaim peace to the earth, and returned with an olive branch, so to our flesh, as it emerges from the font which cleanses from past sin, the Dove of the Holy Spirit flies from Heaven bringing the peace of God.[1] So also S. Ambrose, *De Myst.* 1. iii. 10, 11.[2]

The dove with a cross on its head is interpreted as a symbol of the soul which has received " the seal " in Baptism.

The dove holding a crown represents the soul which has entered the Kingdom of God, and has won a heavenly crown.

Harts Drinking from a Fountain

This, which became a familiar subject in the mosaics, appears in a fresco of the fourth century,

[1] *P.L.* i. col. 1209. [2] *P.L.* xvi. col. 392.

VARIOUS SYMBOLS

in the Catacomb of Marcus and Marcellinus. The reference to Psalm xlii. 1 is evident, and the words which follow make it clearly appropriate to the soul which has been athirst for God, and has come at last to stand in the Presence of God.

S. Jerome, commenting on Ps. xlii. 1, compares the hart quenching its thirst to the catechumen who comes to Baptism, and says that he desires to come to Christ, in Whom is the fount of light, that being cleansed by Baptism he may receive the gift of forgiveness.[1]

In the seventh century in Rome, before the ceremonies of Baptism which took place on Easter Eve, the candidates met to hear lections read from the Old Testament (cf. p. 39). These were concluded with: "As the hart desireth the water-brooks."[2] The prayer said before Baptism asks God to look favourably upon the devotion of those who, like the hart, long for the fountain of water, that by the Sacrament of Baptism this thirst may sanctify them in soul and body.[3]

In consequence of this interpretation the hart was represented in baptisteries, and in the fourth century the Emperor Constantine placed in the baptistery of the Lateran Basilica silver harts with water flowing from their mouths.

THE LAMB

The lamb on the shoulders of the Good Shepherd is a very familiar sight in the early frescoes. Again, when the sheep are seen

---

[1] *P.L.* xxvi. col. 949.   [2] Duchesne, p. 309.
[3] *P.L.* lxxiv. col. 1109.

standing around the Shepherd the significance is still that of the flock of Christ.

Later our Lord Himself was frequently represented as a lamb. On the fourth-century sarcophagus of Junius Bassus small sculptures are introduced showing the lamb striking the rock, multiplying the loaves, and raising Lazarus.

The Lamb of God with a halo appears in the fifth century in the baptistery of the Lateran, and after this time frequently occupies a central position, as may be seen in the apses and triumphal arches of the churches.

Before the introduction of the crucifix with a human figure, i.e. up to the end of the seventh century, the lamb was sometimes placed in the centre of the cross.

The Peacock

This bird, which is found with other birds on pagan tombs, was retained by the Christians as a decoration on sepulchres, partly, no doubt, on account of its splendid appearance, and also because the ancients held the opinion that the flesh of the peacock was incorruptible. Accordingly it became the symbol of immortality to Pagans, Jews, and Christians.

Two peacocks are depicted on a tomb in S. Domitilla which possesses a peculiar interest, the tomb bearing the name Ampliatus. It is possible that this may be the Ampliatus called by S. Paul " my beloved in the Lord " (Rom. xvi. 8). Or it may be a member of his family. The name seems to point to a person of servile origin, but his painted tomb may show that he

VARIOUS SYMBOLS

was a person held in honour in the Church at Rome.

The Phœnix

S. Clement of Rome refers to the belief of the ancient world that the phœnix was a bird, the only one of its kind, in Arabia, where it lived for 500 years, and when it died another phœnix arose out of its ashes.

Do we then think it to be a great and marvellous thing, if the Creator of the universe shall bring about the resurrection of them that have served Him with holiness in the assurance of a good faith, seeing that He showeth to us even by a bird the magnificence of His promise?[1]

And Tertullian:

Must men die once for all, while birds in Arabia are sure of a resurrection?[2]

So also the *Apostolic Constitutions*, v. 7, where the phœnix is said to "furnish an abundant demonstration of the resurrection."[3]

The phœnix, which can be recognized by the nimbus it wears, is often mentioned in Acts of the martyrs; e.g. in the *Acts of S. Cecilia* (martyred towards the end of the second century) it is said that she caused a phœnix to be engraved on the tomb of the martyr Maximus.

It is not habitually found in the most ancient monuments, but was represented with its name on the doors of the ancient basilica of S. Paul,

[1] Lightfoot, p. 19.   [2] *P.L.* ii. col. 811.
[3] *P.G.* i. col. 844.

and it appears on a glass now in the Vatican, seated on a palm-tree, beneath which S. Paul is standing.

The Ship

This subject does not appear very frequently in early Christian art, but in the cemetery of S. Callixtus there is an interesting fresco of the latter part of the second century. A ship is seen tossing on a stormy sea, and nearly covered by the waves. A man is struggling in the water; another man is standing on the deck with arms uplifted in the attitude of prayer, whilst from the sky an outstretched hand is placed upon his head. The ship seems to signify the Church, and the meaning to be that those without the Church are in peril of death, but those within, however great their peril, are protected by the hand of God.

Thus Hippolytus writes:

The sea is the world, in which the Church is set, like a ship tossed in the deep, but not destroyed; for she has with her the skilled Pilot, Christ. And she bears in her midst also the trophy over death, for she carries with her the cross of the Lord. . . . As the wind the Spirit from heaven is present, by Whom those who believe are sealed. . . . She has also mariners on the right hand and on the left, the holy Angels, by whom the Church is always governed and defended. The ladder in her leading up to the sail-yard is the likeness of the sign of the passion of Christ, which brings the faithful to the ascent of Heaven. And the streamers aloft on the sail-yard are the company of prophets, martyrs, and apostles, who are at rest in the kingdom of Christ.[1]

[1] *P.G.* x. col. 778. See also C. Wordsworth, *Hippolytus and the Church of Rome*, pp. 126 f.

VARIOUS SYMBOLS

Tertullian refers to the storm on the Lake of Gennesaret, and says:

The boat sets forth a figure of the Church, which is tossed about in the sea, that is, in the world, by the billows, that is, by persecutions and temptations, whilst the Lord in His patience seems to be asleep, until He is aroused at last by the prayers of the saints, and restrains the world, and restores peace to His people.[1]

[1] *P.L.* i. col. 1214.

CHAPTER XI

THE SACRAMENTS

Baptism. Confirmation. The Eucharist

BAPTISM

WE have noticed the symbols by which Baptism was represented, and the subjects which were regarded as types of Baptism (see pp. 50, 54, 58, 61, 62, 73, 75-79, 88, 89). These will have shown the large place which this Sacrament occupied in the thought of the early Church.

The importance of Baptism in the life of the individual is shown by inscriptions in which it is stated that the deceased person had " received grace," an expression which appears to mean the grace of God received in Baptism. Thus of Julia it is said that she had scarcely received the grace of God ere she was taken in peace, a neophyte. (S. Callixtus.)

The inscription on the sarcophagus of Junius Bassus (fourth century) states that he was prefect of Rome, and died at the age of forty-two, soon after his baptism. Whilst yet " a neophyte he went to God."

Of Simplicius it is recorded that he lived fifty-one years, of which twenty-six were after " his acceptance," i.e. after he had been received into the Church. (Lateran Museum.)

Of Apronianus, who lived twenty-one months,

THE SACRAMENTS

it is said that his grandmother, seeing that he was in peril of death, asked of the Church that he might depart from this world as one of the faithful, i.e. be baptized. (Lateran Museum.)

Victor was not yet baptized, and was still a catechumen when he died at the age of twenty, but the inscription records that he was "a servant of the Lord Jesus Christ." (Lateran Museum.)

In an early fresco in S. Callixtus the Baptism of our Lord is represented with the dove descending upon Him as He comes out of the water. Other frescoes illustrate the manner in which the rite of Baptism was performed in Rome. The baptized person is seen standing in the water, which reaches to his ankles or knees, while water is poured over him. This makes it clear that Baptism by immersion was at any rate not the universal custom. The baptizer is represented with one hand placed on the head of the neophyte, and on one sarcophagus in the Museo delle Terme he is holding in his left hand a roll partly unfolded, which probably signifies the confession of faith made by the neophyte at his Baptism.

This corresponds with the account given of the ceremony of Baptism in *The Church Order of Hippolytus*, i.e. the Use in Rome at the beginning of the third century. When the neophyte is standing in the font, the presbyter is to lay his hand upon his head and to rehearse the Baptismal Creed, first: "Dost thou believe in God the Father Almighty?" and the neophyte shall answer: "Yea, I believe." Then he is baptized the first time. Again he is asked if he believes the teaching of the Creed about Jesus

Christ the Son of God; and lastly if he believes in the Holy Ghost, the Holy Church, and the resurrection of the flesh. Each time he is to answer, " I believe," and is baptized a second and a third time.[1]

Confirmation

Signatus, or *consignatus*, in an inscription appears to denote the reception of the sign made upon the forehead in Confirmation.

As Confirmation usually followed immediately upon Baptism, it is not to be expected that there should be many references to it as a distinct ceremony.

The Church Order of Hippolytus directs that the neophyte is to come from the baptistery into the church, and the Bishop is to lay his hand upon him and pray, and then anoint his head and make the sign upon his forehead.[1]

An inscription, of which only a copy remains, speaks of the place where the chief pastor with his right hand makes the sign on the sheep of his flock when they have been cleansed in the heavenly stream. They are summoned to come where the Holy Spirit calls them to receive His gifts; and having been signed with the cross, to learn to escape from the tempests of this world.[2]

The Eucharist

This is represented in many ways, and sometimes in connexion with the Agape, i.e. the

[1] Connolly, *The So-called Egyptian Church Order : Texts and Studies*, vol. viii, No. 4, 1916, pp. 184, 185.
[2] De Rossi, *Inscr. Christ*. ii. p. 139.

THE SACRAMENTS

common meal at which Christians met in token of their fellowship, and which it seems was at first combined with the celebration of the Holy Eucharist, even as the Last Supper with the first Eucharist.

What was the connexion in the minds of the early Christians between the Eucharist and the faithful departed so that it should be considered suitable to represent it on their tombs?

The connexion was a very close one, for the Eucharist was believed to bring eternal life not

EUCHARISTIC SCENE. IN S. CALLIXTUS. SECOND CENTURY.

only to the soul of the communicant, but to his body also.

So S. Ignatius:

Breaking one bread which is the medicine of immortality, and the antidote that we should not die but live for ever in Jesus Christ.[1]

And S. Irenæus:

How say they that the flesh passes into corruption and partakes not of life which is nourished with the Body of the Lord and with His Blood? ... As bread from the earth receiving the summons of God is no longer common bread but Eucharist, made up of two things, an earthly and a heavenly, so also our

[1] Lightfoot, p. 111.

bodies partaking of the Eucharist are no longer corruptible, but having the hope of the resurrection to eternity.[1]

Again :

Since therefore the cup which is mingled, and the bread which is made, receiveth the Word of God, and the Eucharist becometh the Body of Christ, and of these the substance of our flesh groweth and subsisteth, how can they say that the flesh is not capable of the gift of God, which is life eternal, that flesh which is nourished from the Body and Blood of the Lord, and is a member of Him?

As the vine planted in the ground bears fruit in its season, and the corn of wheat falling into the earth and mouldering is raised up by the Spirit of God and becomes the Eucharist, which is the Body and Blood of Christ—

so also our bodies nourished thereby and put in the ground and dissolved therein, shall rise again in their own time, the Word of God granting them resurrection to the glory of God.[2]

The Liturgy of the Nestorians has the Invocation :

May there come ... Thine Holy Spirit and rest upon this offering of Thy servants, and bless and hallow it that it be to us ... for the pardon of offences and the remission of sins, and for the great hope of resurrection from the dead, and for new life in the kingdom of Heaven with all those who have been well-pleasing in Thy sight.[3]

---

[1] *P.G.* vii. col. 1028.
[2] Ibid., col. 1125.
[3] Brightman, *Eastern Liturgies*, p. 287.

THE SACRAMENTS

Moreover, from the second century, at any rate, it was customary to offer oblations for the faithful departed on the anniversaries of their death. The day of a martyr's death was called his birthday, as the Smyrneans, speaking of the resting-place where they had laid the ashes of their martyred Bishop, S. Polycarp, declare their intention of gathering there to celebrate the birthday of his martyrdom in gladness and joy.[1]

So Tertullian speaks of the oblations which are offered year by year to commemorate the birthdays of the departed.[2]

And S. Cyprian:

> We always offer sacrifices for them, as often as we annually celebrate and commemorate the passions and death-days of the martyrs.[3]

Pseudo-Cyprian speaks of Christ and the Angels and the martyrs as present at the table of the Lord.[4]

S. Cyril of Jerusalem says that it was the custom in his Church after the Oblation of the sacred gifts to—

> make mention of those who are fallen asleep, first of patriarchs, prophets, apostles, martyrs, that God would at their prayers and intercessions receive our supplication; then on behalf of our holy fathers and Bishops and of all who have fallen asleep before us, believing that it will be the greatest benefit to the souls on behalf of whom our prayer

[1] Lightfoot, p. 196.
[2] *P.L.* ii. col. 78.
[3] *P.L.* iv. col. 331.
[4] *P.L.* iv. 910.

is offered whilst the holy and most awful Sacrifice is lying before us.[1]

On the occasion of the commemoration of a martyr it was natural that the gathering should be held at his place of burial, and the Oblation be offered on his tomb. The modern altar still preserves the shape of a tomb.

One of the very earliest symbols of the Eucharist appears in the Crypt of Lucina (early second century).[2] Here are two pictures, in each of which a fish is represented on a green ground with a basket containing loaves, five in one and six in the other. Through the basket is seen what appears to be a vessel of glass, holding red wine. Bread, fish, and wine are the regular symbols of the Eucharist.

S. Jerome writes: " No one is richer than he who bears the Body of the Lord in a wicker basket, and His Blood in a glass." [3]

S. Paulinus of Nola calls Christ " the true Bread and the Fish of the living water." [4]

Several frescoes show a number of people, often seven, seated at a crescent-shaped table.[5] (S. Callixtus.) In accordance with the custom of the time they are represented as resting with the left arm on a long cushion which is placed on the table. In front there stands in some pictures the small tripod table upon which the dishes were placed before being handed by the servants to the diners. The dishes in these frescoes contain loaves and fishes. A row of baskets, often seven or twelve in number, points

[1] *P.G.* xxxiii. col. 1116.
[2] See p. 48.
[3] *P.L.* xxii. col. 1085.
[4] *P.L.* lxi. col. 213.
[5] See p. 97.

THE SACRAMENTS

to the connexion with the miraculous feeding of the multitudes.

In one fresco in S. Callixtus a variation appears. The diners are nude and there are no baskets. This therefore is thought to represent the repast of the disciples by the lake (S. John xxi.).

S. Augustine regards the seven disciples as types of all the faithful in the communion of the Sacrament. "Piscis assus Christus est passus": "The broiled fish is Christ Who has suffered. With Him the Church is united for the participation of eternal blessedness."[1]

In a few of the other frescoes in which a banquet is represented (e.g. SS. Pietro e Marcellino) there appear two figures of attendants with inscriptions which designate them as Agape and Irene, i.e. Love and Peace, and the words addressed to them by the guests are given: "Bring warm water. Mix for us." Wine was habitually drunk mixed with warm water. Justin[2] and other early writers expressly state that water was mixed with the wine at the Eucharist.

In these frescoes the Agape of the faithful with Love and Peace in attendance foreshadows the Heavenly Feast (S. Luke xxii. 30).

The *Passio SS. Mariani et Jacobi*, who suffered martyrdom in A.D. 259, relates that Jacobus had a vision shortly before his death in which he saw another martyr preparing a splendid and joyful feast. Being brought

[1] *P.L.* xxxv. col. 1966.
[2] *Apol.* i. 65.

thither as to an Agape, he met a lad who had been martyred three days earlier wearing a wreath of roses and holding a palm-branch, who said to him: " Rejoice and be glad, for to-morrow you will dine with us."[1]

A fresco in S. Priscilla, of the beginning of the second century, shows a table at which are reclining five men and a woman. At the head of the table a seventh person is seated; before him are set a cup, a dish with five loaves, and another with two fishes. He is represented as stretching his hand towards them as if preparing to dispense them. Hence the name *Fractio Panis* by which this picture is known. There are also three baskets of loaves on one side of the picture, and four on the other side.

In one of the Chapels of the Sacraments in S. Callixtus is a fresco in which a fish and a loaf of bread are seen set on a small tripod table, at one side of which a man clad in a pallium is standing with his hand stretched over the fish. On the other side of the table stands an Orante, typifying the communion of the soul with God in the Holy Eucharist.

Later the consecration is represented in another way. We have noticed (on pp. 73, 77) the representations of Christ touching with His rod the six water-pots and the baskets of loaves set before Him, or standing with His hands placed upon the loaves and the fishes. This corresponds to the conception of the offering of the Eucharistic elements which Christ by His

[1] *Passio SS. Mariani et Jacobi*, Pio Franchi de' Cavalieri, p. 60.

EUCHARISTIC SCENE.
WITH PRIEST AND ORANTE.
IN *S. CALLIXTUS*.
2ND CENTURY.

facing p. 102.

THE SACRAMENTS

divine power makes to be His Body and His Blood.

Accordingly Justin speaks of them as follows :

> We do not receive them as common bread or common drink, but just as Jesus Christ our Saviour was made flesh by the word of God, and had both flesh and blood for our salvation, so also we have been taught that the food over which thanksgiving has been made [or, which was blessed] by the prayer of the word that is from Him, and from which our flesh and our blood receive nourishment by assimilation, is both the flesh and the blood of that Jesus Who was made flesh.[1]

The words of S. Irenæus in this connexion have been already quoted (p. 98).

A Greek inscription which is thought to belong to the early part of the third century was found at Autun. It consists of verses of which the first six lines appear to refer to Eucharistic communion under the symbolism of the Fish. The initial letters of the first five lines form the Greek word ΙΧΘΥΣ. The last lines show that the inscription was an epitaph, and possibly they were added to make it suitable for this purpose. As some part of the text is defaced, attempts have been made to restore it conjecturally. This, e.g., is how it is translated in Marucchi's *Christian Epigraphy*, p. 125 :

> Thou the divine offspring of the heavenly ΙΧΘΥΣ, keep a pure heart while thou receivest the source of God-given waters, immortal gift to mortals. Comfort thy soul, O friend, with the ever-flowing

[1] *Apol.* i. 66.

waters of wealth-giving wisdom, and receive the honey-sweet food of the Redeemer of the Saints; eat in thy hunger, holding ΙΧΘΥΣ in thy hands. Satisfy thyself with ΙΧΘΥΣ. My desire is to Thee, my Saviour; to Thee I pray, Thou Light of the dead. Ascandius, father, my heart's beloved, and with thee my darling mother and my brethren in the peace of ΙΧΘΥΣ. Remember thy Pectorius.

CHAPTER XII

LATER CHRISTIAN ART

Christ enthroned. The Mosaics : S. Costanza, SS. Cosma e Damiano, S. John Lateran, S. Clemente. The Victory of the Faith.

CHRIST ASCENDED AND EXALTED

IN frescoes of the fourth century, or possibly rather earlier, our Lord begins to be represented as seated among the twelve Apostles, as the Master teaching His disciples.

When we come to the close of the period of art in the Catacombs a fresco is found which anticipates the Christian art of the succeeding ages. This fresco (in SS. Pietro e Marcellino) is of the end of the fourth or beginning of the fifth century, and illustrates the profound change which Christian art had undergone since the first and second centuries when our Lord was represented in the simplest fashion as a youthful shepherd. In this later fresco our Lord, no longer beardless, appears enthroned wearing a halo bearing the ☧ between A and ω (Alpha and Omega). On His right stands S. Paul, on His left S. Peter. Beneath them the Lamb of God is standing on a hill whence four rivers flow, with Iordas (Jordan) written above.

The halo of the Lamb also bears ☧.

Two saints on either side stand with their hands stretched out towards the Lamb.

EARLY CHRISTIANS OF ROME

We have here some of the main features of the mosaics which adorn the apses and triumphal arches of the ancient churches of Rome.

Again, on the sarcophagus of Junius Bassus Christ appears enthroned, whilst beneath His feet is a figure holding a veil spread out above his head. This is thought to represent the firmament above which Christ is seated. On either side stands an Apostle holding a roll. A sarcophagus with a somewhat similar design is in the Lateran Museum. It has been interpreted as representing Christ in glory committing His authority or His new Law to the Apostles, and in some examples of this kind, to one of the Apostles. We have seen that in the early tradition and art of Christian Rome S. Peter is always associated with S. Paul, but in course of time he came to occupy a position more peculiar to himself. In the fifth century there appears a new subject, viz. S. Peter receiving the keys from Christ. If this is represented in one fresco of the Catacombs, it does not appear to have become usual till the end of the sixth century.

A passage in Duchesne's *Christian Worship* is of interest in this connexion (p. 301). He describes a ceremony which formed part of the preparation for Baptism in Rome at any rate about the seventh century, and probably much earlier. This was the *Traditio Symboli*. On the appointed day the candidates were solemnly instructed in the Creed and the Christian Law, " the most holy Law," as it is called.

This simple, but very imposing, ceremony must

LATER CHRISTIAN ART

have produced a lively impression on the candidates for Baptism. I am inclined to believe that this ceremony finds artistic expression in the representation of the giving of the Law which we find on many early Christian monuments, such as pictures, sarcophagi, decorated vases, and especially the apsidal mosaics of the basilicas. Christ is there depicted as seated on a splendid throne placed on the summit of a mountain from whence flow the four rivers of Paradise. Around Him are assembled the Apostles. S. Peter, their chief, receives from the hands of the Saviour a book—emblem of the Christian Law—on which is inscribed DOMINUS LEGEM DAT, or some similar device. Above this group there appear in the azure of the sky the four symbolical animals with the four books of the Gospel. I would not take upon myself to say that this scene was expressly depicted from the ritual of the *Traditio Legis Christianæ*, but there is such a striking resemblance between the two things that the likeness could not fail to have been remarked. Many of the faithful, when casting their eyes upon the paintings which decorated the apses of their churches, must have had thus brought before them one of the most beautiful ceremonies of their initiation.

MOSAICS

In the mausoleum of S. Costanza are found the earliest Christian mosaics, dating from the fourth century. In one of these a figure, which may be that of Christ, is seated on a globe and holding out some object to a figure by His side. It is thought that this may represent the giving of the Law to Moses; but if so, it seems to be unique of its kind. In another of these mosaics Christ is standing between two Apostles, to one of whom He is giving a scroll inscribed DOMINUS

PACEM DAT. Streams are flowing from beneath
His feet, and four lambs are coming towards
them from some buildings at either side of the
picture, a feature which is commonly repeated
in the later mosaics. In these pictures Christ
alone has a halo.

The mosaics which adorn the Church of SS.
Cosma e Damiano demand particular attention
as being perhaps the finest and most impressive
of all the ancient mosaics in the churches of
Rome, and as showing in a remarkable way the
development of the ideas which have been
noticed in the Catacombs and on the sarcophagi.
These mosaics date from the time of Pope
Felix IV, A.D. 526–30.

On the triumphal arch the Lamb appears on
a jewelled throne surrounded by seven candle-
sticks, and surmounted by a cross. On the step
of the throne is a book with seals attached. In
the apse the Saviour, a majestic figure, is represented standing on clouds of radiant glory.
His right hand is raised, in His left He holds
a roll. On either side stand S. Paul and S.
Peter presenting to Christ the two saints to
whom the church is dedicated, SS. Cosma and
Damiano. They were martyrs, and hold crowns
in their hands. Another martyr, S. Theodore,
and Pope Felix stand one on each side of the
picture by palm trees with bunches of dates.
On one tree a phœnix with a star-shaped nimbus
is sitting. Below this scene is the River
Jordan; and beneath, the Lamb of God is
standing on a rock whence four streams are
flowing with the names inscribed: *Geon, Fyson,
Tigris, Eufrata.* On either side of the Lamb is

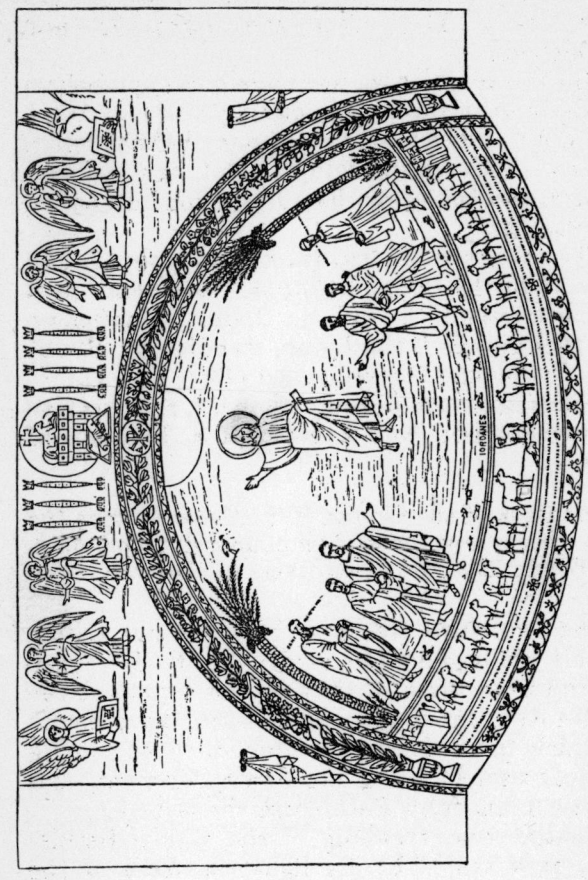

THE APSE AND TRIUMPHAL ARCH OF SS. COSMA E DAMIANO, ROME.
From *The Dictionary of Christian Antiquities*, vol. ii.

EARLY CHRISTIANS OF ROME

a line of sheep, six coming from a city at one side of the picture, and six from a city on the other side. The cities are Jerusalem and Bethlehem.

In these mosaics we meet again the symbolism of the earlier days, the sheep, the palm trees, and the four rivers of Paradise, and the phœnix, symbol of the resurrection. But new features appear, and the symbolism has gained an added significance.

The influence of Rev. iv. and v. is seen in the mosaics of the triumphal arch, " the Lamb as it had been slain "; and the Lamb standing on the rock recalls " the Lamb standing on Mount Zion " amongst the redeemed (Rev. xiv. 1).

The four rivers flowing from the rock receive an explanation from a verse of S. Paulinus of Nola:

The Rock of the Church Himself stands upon the rock whence flow the four fountains with loud voice, the Evangelists, the living rivers of Christ.[1]

The two cities are those in which our Lord's earthly life began and ended. The twelve sheep coming from them, if they do not represent the twelve Apostles, may symbolize the two elements of which the Church is composed, those coming from Jerusalem being the Jewish element, and those coming from Bethlehem the Gentiles.

S. Augustine, speaking of the star of Bethlehem, says that " by its light the faith of the Gentiles was begun." [2]

---

[1] *P.L.* lxi. col. 336.
[2] *P.L.* xxxviii. col. 1031. Cf. p. 71.

LATER CHRISTIAN ART

Other sheep I have, which are not of this fold: them also I must bring ... and they shall be one flock.

These two elements in the Church are represented in a fifth-century mosaic in the Church of S. Sabina by two women with the inscription: " The Church of the Circumcision "; " The Church of the Gentiles."

The subjects which we have seen in SS. Cosma and Damiano are met with again and again in other mosaics in the churches of Rome. In some, however, other features of the more ancient art appear, and therefore may be briefly noticed, though these mosaics take us beyond the time which it is the purpose of this book to consider.

In the apse of S. John Lateran the central place is occupied by a cross standing on a hill, and above the Dove is seen descending. Thence flow the four mystic rivers, and by them two harts are standing apparently as symbolizing the desire for Baptism, which would accord with the use of this symbolism to which reference has been made. See p. 89.

In the very fine mosaics which adorn the apse of S. Clemente the harts are also represented drinking from the four rivers. Around the figure on the cross above are twelve doves. A description given by S. Paulinus of Nola of a mosaic in his church makes it probable that the doves in S. Clemente represent the twelve Apostles.[1]

This mosaic is remarkable for the beautiful

[1] *P.L.* lxi. col. 336.

EARLY CHRISTIANS OF ROME

tracery of the great Vine which, springing from the foot of the cross, occupies the whole space of the apse. Birds, flowers, and fruit appear among its branches.

The vine is no novelty in Christian art. It had been employed as a decoration from early times, in part doubtless as a heritage from pagan art. Even in the fourth-century mosaics of S. Costanza the design of the artists is to portray the familiar scenes of the vintage, rather than to set forth a piece of Christian symbolism. But in S. Clemente the inscription on the apse leaves no doubt of its significance.[1] The Vine represents the Church, which owes its life and vigour to the Cross.

These words fitly sum up the story told by the early monuments. The mosaics belong to another world, a world in which the victory of the Church was manifestly secure. The early monuments will have helped us to understand how the victory was won, and to find the answer to the question with which our inquiry began : how was it possible for the Christian message to prevail against the hostile forces of the pagan world ?

For notwithstanding all hindrances without and all weaknesses within, the fact of the Church remains. That is a fact which has to be accounted for, and can only be fully explained by the inherent power of the Faith of which she was the witness. We have seen of what substance that Faith was made, not such a Faith as timidly questions whether we can know any-

---

[1] Ecclesiam Christi viti similabimus isti,
    Quam lex arentem sed crux fecit esse virentem.

LATER CHRISTIAN ART

thing of the life hereafter, but a Faith grounded on the assurance of God's power to guard the souls and bodies of His people in life, in death, and after death; on the conviction that the eternal life given by Christ and begun in the fellowship of the Church here will be continued in communion with God and with the saints hereafter. It was a Faith persuaded that Christ did not come into the world and die upon the Cross in order to relieve men from the necessity of peril, toil, and suffering, but in order to redeem them from sin and to lead them in the path of sacrifice.

Thus " they overcame because of the blood of the Lamb, and because of the word of their testimony; and they loved not their life even unto death."

" Here is the patience and the faith of the saints."

APPENDIX

THE NERONIAN PERSECUTION AFTER THE FIRE AT ROME, A.D. 64

BUT all human efforts, all the lavish gifts of the emperor, and the propitiations of the gods, did not banish the sinister belief that the conflagration was the result of an order. Consequently, to get rid of the report, Nero fastened the guilt and inflicted the most exquisite tortures on a class hated for their abominations, called Christians by the populace. Christus, from whom the name had its origin, suffered the extreme penalty during the reign of Tiberius at the hands of one of our procurators, Pontius Pilatus, and a most mischievous superstition, thus checked for the moment, again broke out not only in Judæa, the first source of the evil, but even in Rome, where all things hideous and shameful from every part of the world find their centre and become popular. Accordingly, an arrest was first made of all who pleaded guilty; then, upon their information, an immense multitude was convicted, not so much of the crime of firing the city, as of hatred against mankind. Mockery of every sort was added to their deaths. Covered with the skins of beasts, they were torn by dogs and perished, or were nailed to crosses, or were doomed to the flames and burnt, to serve as a nightly illumination when daylight had expired. Nero offered his gardens for the spectacle, and was exhibiting a show in the circus, while he mingled with the people in the dress of a charioteer or stood aloft on a car. Hence, even for

APPENDIX

criminals who deserve extreme and exemplary punishment, there arose a feeling of compassion; for it was not, as it seemed, for the public good, but to glut one man's cruelty, that they were being destroyed.

CHURCH AND BRODRIBB, *Annals of Tacitus*, xv. 44.

(by permission of Messrs. Macmillan).

BIBLIOGRAPHY

RELIGIONS OF ROME

Angus, S., *The Mystery-religions*, 1925.
Cumont, F., *Mysteries of Mithra*, 1903.
Cumont, F., *Les Religions orientales dans le paganisme romain*, 1909.
Warde Fowler, W., *The Religious Experience of the Roman People*, 1911.
Warde Fowler, W., Article on " Roman Religion " in the *Encyclopædia of Religion and Ethics*.

JEWISH CATACOMBS

Garrucci, R., *Cimitero degli antichi Ebrei*, 1862.
Jewish Encyclopædia.

CHRISTIAN ARCHÆOLOGY

Cabrol, F., and H. Leclercq, *Monumenta ecclesiæ liturgica*, vol. i, 1900–1902.
De Rossi, G. B., *Inscriptiones christianæ urbis Romæ* (begun by De Rossi).
De Rossi, G. B., *Roma Sotterranea*, compiled from the works of De Rossi by J. Spencer Northcote and W. R. Brownlow, 2 vols., 1869.
Dictionnaire d'archéologie chrétienne et de liturgie, edited by Dom Cabrol (not yet complete).
Dictionary of Christian Antiquities, edited by Smith and Cheetham, 2 vols., 1875, 1880.
Duchesne, L., *Christian Worship*, English edition.
Leclercq, H., *Manuel d'archéologie chrétienne*, 2 vols., 1907.

BIBLIOGRAPHY

Marucchi, O., *Eléments d'archéologie chrétienne*, 2 vols., 1899, 1900.
Marucchi, O., *Christian Epigraphy*, 1912.
Nuovo Bullettino d'archeologia cristiana.
Wilpert, J., *Principienfragen der christlichen Archäologie*, 1889.

CHRISTIAN CATACOMBS

Marucchi, O., *Le Catacombe romane*, 1903.
Wilpert, J., *Malereien der Katakomben Roms*, 1903. (The first vol. contains the German text, the second vol. a very large number of reproductions in colour of the paintings in the Catacombs.)

INSCRIPTIONS AND SARCOPHAGI

Grousset, R., *Catalogue des sarcophages chrétiens de Rome qui ne se trouvent point au Musée du Lateran*, 1885.
Marucchi, O., *I monumenti del Museo Cristiano Pio Lateranense*, 1910. (Includes reproductions of many sarcophagi and inscriptions preserved in the Lateran Museum.)

MOSAICS

de Jouy, H. Barbet, *Les Mosaiques chrétiennes des basiliques et des églises de Rome*, 1857.
De Rossi, G. B., *Musaici cristiani*, 1872—1875. (Contains reproductions in colour of many mosaics in the churches of Rome.)
Fontana, G., *Raccolta delle migliori chiese di Roma e suburbane*, 1838.

BIBLIOGRAPHY

TRANSLATIONS OF GREEK AND LATIN TEXTS

The Ante-Nicene Christian Library.

Eusebius, *Ecclesiastical History*, translated by A. C. McGiffert, 1890.

Eusebius, *Ecclesiastical History*, translated by H. J. Lawlor and J. E. L. Oulton, 1927.

Kidd, B. J., *Documents illustrative of the History of the Church*, 2 vols., 1920, 1923.

ORIGINAL TEXTS IN GREEK AND LATIN

Migne, *Patrologia Græca* = *P.G.* in notes.
Migne, *Patrologia Latina* = *P.L.* in notes.
Corpus Scriptorum Ecclesiasticorum Latinorum.

GREEK TEXT WITH ENGLISH TRANSLATION

Lightfoot, J. B., *The Apostolic Fathers*, 1 vol., 1891.

*Made and Printed in Great Britain
by Hazell, Watson & Viney Ld.
London and Aylesbury*

DATE DUE			
MAY 12 '70			
GAYLORD			PRINTED IN U.S.A.